KU-673-822

CHINESE
Cook Book

AMY WONG

MEREHURST

Published in 1995 by Merehurst Limited
Ferry House, 51–57 Lacy Road, Putney, London SW15 1PR

Reprinted 1996

Copyright © 1995 Merehurst Limited

ISBN 1–85391–421–5

All rights reserved. No part of this publication may be
reproduced, stored in a retrieval system, or transmitted in
any form or by any means, electronic, mechanical,
photocopying or otherwise, without the prior written
permission of the copyright owner.

A catalogue record for this book is available from the
British Library

Series Editor: Valerie Barrett
Design: Clive Dorman
Illustrations: Keith Sparrow

Typeset by Clive Dorman & Co.
Colour Separation by P&W Graphics Pty Ltd, Singapore
Printed and bound in Great Britain by
Mackays of Chatham PLC, Chatham, Kent

RECIPE NOTES

Indicates dishes that cook in under 35 minutes

● Follow one set of measurements only, do not mix metric and imperial

● All spoon measures are level

● Always taste and adjust seasonings to suit your own preferences

Indicates dishes that are suitable for vegetarians

CONTENTS

INTRODUCTION

There is an old Chinese proverb that says, 'To the ruler, people are heaven; to the people, food is heaven.' Food has often been scarce in China, and hunger an ever-present threat, so food is precious to the Chinese and treated with great care and respect. The Chinese have a long history of culinary development, and as in other aspects of their lives, they have always sought perfection. They value the body, and so diet and cooking are very important to them.

When cooking Chinese food, the art lies not in the basic cooking skills needed, but in the choice and blending of ingredients to give a mixture of compatible yet contrasting appearances, colours, aromas, flavours, and textures. Everything should be fresh and clean and there should always be sweet, sour, bitter, salty and hot tastes in a Chinese meal.

A traditional meal consists of two parts called 'Fan-cai'. This simply means that one half consists of 'Fan' or the staple grain such as rice, noodles or dumplings, and the other half consists of the 'cai' which is anything else such as fish, meat, poultry and vegetable dishes. A typical meal consists of a soup, one 'Fan' dish and three or four 'cai' dishes.

Each dish should be varied but complementary. For example, a spicy dish with a mild one, a crisp dish with a soft one, a moist dish with a dry one and so on. The more people there are at the table, the more varied the dishes can be. That is one of the reasons Chinese food is perfect for special occasions or groups of people eating together.

Here you will find lots of your favourite recipes such as Sweet and Sour Pork, Peking Duck, Spring Rolls, Special Fried Rice and many more. All the recipes use ingredients easily obtainable in supermarkets or specialist food shops.

PREPARATION

As Chinese food is eaten with chopsticks or soup spoons, it is obviously easier to manage if cut into small pieces. This also enables the food to be cooked very quickly and evenly, which means the colour and flavour is preserved. It is usual to cut all the ingredients that are together in one dish, into uniformly small pieces.

Meat and vegetables may be cut into chunks of about 2 cm (¾ inch), or small dice of 6 – 12.5 mm (¼-½ inch), long narrow strips of 2.5 x 3 x 3.75 mm (1 x ⅛ x 1½ inches) or fine shreds of 3 x 3 x 3.75 mm (⅛ x ⅛ x 1½ inches). Meat is sliced across the grain and when wafer-thin slices are needed it helps if the meat is frozen first. Allow the meat to defrost after slicing or shredding before cooking. Vegetables are often cut diagonally so as to increase the surface area that comes into contact with hot oil or pan and this ensures fast, even cooking.

EQUIPMENT

Chinese cooking requires very few utensils and most of those are likely to be in your kitchen already. The one thing that you may need to buy, especially if you want to make lots of stir-fried dishes, is a wok.

The Wok

The wok evolved many centuries ago and is an all-purpose cooking pan as it can be used for stir-frying, steaming and deep-frying. It is a circular, round-bottomed steel pan with either one single handle or two small handles, one on either side.

You can buy woks in various sizes, but a good average one would be about 35 cm (14 inches) in diameter. Traditional round-bottomed woks need an adaptor ring or hob stand unless you have a gas cooker that will cradle the rounded bottom. Woks with a slightly flattened base are available for electric stoves. They can now be bought in stainless steel, aluminium and non-stick varieties. The double-handled versions are good for deep-frying, braising, boiling and steaming, and the single-handled woks are good for stir-frying.

Before using a traditional steel wok, it should be washed in hot, soapy water, to remove the protective coating of oil. Wipe clean and then rub 1 tablespoon of vegetable oil and 1 teaspoon of salt over the surface. Heat until it begins to smoke and then remove from the heat and allow to cool. Wipe with kitchen paper. After use, woks should only be washed with water: don't use soap or scouring pads, and always rinse and dry well. After a time a black patina builds up, which, according to the Chinese, improves the flavour of the food.

A modern wok often comes with several 'attachments'. A wire or metal rack which fits inside to use for steaming, a large domed lid, and a steel stand. Also there may be two flat ladles or wok spatulas, (one of which is perforated), a wire strainer for use when deep-frying, and a pair of long chopsticks for stirring.

Steaming Baskets

These are circular wooden cylinders with a criss-cross lattice of bamboo inside.

The most useful-sized bamboo steamer for home cooking is 20 cm (8 inch) in diameter. The steamer is designed so that several can be stacked one on top of another and so multiple cooking can take place. The food that takes the longest to cook is placed in the bottom steamer, with the food requiring the shortest cooking time in the top steamer. Bamboo steamers are available from Oriental and Asian food shops.

Cleaver

Chinese cooks use a cleaver as a multi-purpose tool, for

chopping, cutting, crushing and shredding. You can, of course, just use a good sharp knife, but Chinese cleavers are very easy to use with a little practice and are worth buying if you cook a lot of Chinese or Oriental dishes. They can be bought in varying sizes and weights.

Chopping Board

Chinese cooking involves a lot of chopping and cutting, and a good board is essential. A traditional Chinese choping block is a cross section of a hardwood tree trunk. They come in various diameters but must be at least 5 cm (2 inches) thick. A new block should be seasoned well with vegetable oil to prevent splitting. After use it should not be washed in water or with soap – simply scrape clean with the cleaver or a sharp knife and wipe with a clean cloth wrung out in hot water. Alternatively, you can use a large rectangular board of hard wood or an acrylic chopping board, but make sure the board is thick if you intend to use a Chinese cleaver.

COOKING METHODS

Stir-frying

To stir-fry, heat the oil in the wok until very hot. Add the ingredients, and using a large, long-handled wooden or metal wok spatula, continually toss and stir the food in the hot pan. The heat is greatest at the base of the pan, and so by tossing and stirring the food, all sides are quickly sealed and all the juices and flavours are kept in. Stir-fried food should be served at once.

Steaming

This can be done in the wok. A special wire or metal rack is put in the wok and water is poured in the bottom to within 2.5 cm (1 inch) of the rack. The water is brought to the boil and the bamboo steamer placed on top. Place the lid on the wok and leave to steam, checking now and then that there is enough water in the pan. Alternatively, you can fit the steamer on to the top of a saucepan containing boiling water. If you don't have bamboo steamers then use a heat-proof plate on the rack in the wok.

Deep-frying

This can be done in a deep-fat fryer or a saucepan with a wire basket, or use a wok and a flat, round, wire strainer for removing cooked items.

Other methods

Cooking techniques such as stewing, braising, boiling and roasting are also used in Chinese cooking but they are carried out in the same way as we would do it.

INGREDIENTS

Agar agar: This is an extract of seaweed and is used in Asian and vegetarian cooking as a substitute for gelatine. It comes in either small transparent strips of various colours or powder form. When dissolved in water over a low heat, agar agar blends with water and on cooling sets to a jelly. It is very important that agar agar is completely dissolved before cooking. Stir in boiling water and simmer over a low heat for 5 minutes. It will set in about an hour at room temperature.

Bamboo shoots: These are only available in cans in this country, and should be rinsed and drained before using. Can be bought in larger supermarkets.

Bean curd sheets: Available from Oriental food stores and some health food shops, this is the skin that forms during the making of tofu (bean curd). It is skimmed off the boiled mixture then dried. It is sometimes called bean curd skin.

Bean sauces and pastes: There are a huge range of bean

sauces and pastes available in Oriental food stores. These include yellow and black bean sauce, black bean garlic sauce and chilli bean sauce. Most are made from puréed soy beans with various seasonings added.

Bean sprouts: These are the small white shoots of the mung bean plant. They are widely available fresh from most supermarkets. The canned varieties do not have the crunchy texture of the fresh ones.

Chilli paste: Sometimes called 'Szechwan paste' it is made from hot peppers, salt and garlic and can be bought in Chinese supermarkets.

Chinese barbecued pork or Chinese roast pork (char siew): Available from Oriental food stores that sell meat. Pork fillet is marinated in a soy sauce mixture then roasted at a high temperature. The result is a red coloured pork with a crusty surface. If unavailable, roast pork can be used instead.

Chinese leaves: Sometimes called 'Petsai', these have tightly-packed, pale green leaves with jagged edges. When eaten raw they have a flavour that is a cross between lettuce and cabbage, and their crisp crunchy texture makes them ideal for stir-fries.

Chinese sausage (lap cheong): These are highly flavoured sausages made with chopped lean and fatty pork and spices. About the size of frankfurters, they taste similar to salami and add a 'wind dried' flavour to a dish. They are available from Oriental food stores. If unavailable, any spicy sausage can be substituted.

Cloud ears: These black fungi, also known as wood ears, are available from Oriental food stores. Like dried Chinese mushrooms they have to be soaked in hot water until soft before using. If unavailable, dried Chinese mushrooms can be used instead.

Coconut milk: This can be purchased in a number of forms – canned, as a long-life product in cartons or as a powder to which you add water. Once opened, it has a short life and should be used with a day or so.

Coriander: Also known as Chinese parsley or cilantro, this is an attractive herb whose leaves are widely used in chinese cookery.

Dried chestnuts: Available from Oriental food stores, these should not be confused with water chestnuts. Before using, soak dried chestnuts in hot water until soft – this will take about 30 minutes. Then using the tip of a sharp knife carefully remove the skin.

Dried Chinese mushrooms: These are fairly expensive, but a few will add a unique flavour to any dish. To use dried mushrooms, place mushrooms in a bowl, cover with boiling water and set aside to soak for 20 minutes or until soft. Squeeze out excess liquid, remove tough stem and use as required. For added flavour, the soaking liquid is often added to dishes.

Dried shrimps: These are highly salted, dried shrimps and are available in Chinese supermarkets.

Five spice powder: A mixture of five aromatic spices – cinnamon, clove, fennel, star anise and Szechwan pepper. Available in ground form in most large supermarkets.

Ginger juice: This is simply the juice extracted from fresh ginger. If a large quantity is required use a juicer to extract the juice. For small quantities the easiest way to extract the juice is by using a garlic crusher.

Green mung pea flour: Often labelled as 'tepung juan kwe' this is available from Oriental food stores. It is made from the tiny green peas which are sprouted to form bean sprouts. If unavailable, arrowroot is a suitable substitute. However, the flavour will be a little different.

Hoisin sauce: Also known as Chinese barbecue sauce, this is a thick, dark brown sauce made from soy beans, vinegar, sugar, spices and other flavourings. It has a sweet spicy flavour and is mainly used in southern Chinese cooking.

Noodles: Chinese noodles can be bought fresh from Chinese food stores, but many dried varieties are available in large supermarkets.

Egg noodles – these range from flat broad ribbons to long narrow strands.

Cellophane noodles – sometimes called 'bean thread' or 'transparent' noodles these are made from mung bean flour and can be bought in Chinese, Japanese and some large supermarkets.

Rice noodles – range from very thick to very fine or vermicelli type noodles which are good for deep frying.

Oyster sauce: This is a thick brown concentrated sauce made from soy sauce in which oysters have been simmered. Available in bottles in most large supermarkets.

Pak choi: Also called Chinese cabbage, these small leafy bunches do not resemble cabbage. The white or pale green stalks are tightly bunched and about halfway up, the midgreen oval leaves appear. The chopped stalks and leaves can be eaten raw or cooked.

Pandan essence: Made from the leaves of the pandanus or screw pine, this essence is used as a flavouring and colouring in Asian and Indian cooking. It is pale-green in colour and has a warm nutlike flavour. It is available as a powder or a liquid. Vanilla essence can be used in its place but the colour and flavour of the dish will be different. Food flavoured with pandan essence has a distinctive green colour. If you wish to retain this colour and pandan essence is unavailable, vanilla essence and green food colouring can be used instead.

Plum sauce: A popular dipping sauce, plum sauce is made from plums preserved in vinegar, sugar, chillies and spices.

Red bean curd: This is pressed bean curd which has been fermented with rice wine, salt, spices and red-dyed rice. It has a pungent flavour and is available in jars or cans from Oriental food stores.

Rice wine: Chinese rice wine is made from glutinous rice and is sometimes called Yellow wine because of its colour. It can be bought in Chinese supermarkets, but a dry or medium sherry makes an acceptable substitute.

Saffron: Saffron is the most expensive spice in the world. It is the dried stigmas of the flowers of the saffron crocus. Saffron imparts a distinctive aroma, a bitter honey-like taste and a strong yellow colour to food. It is better to buy the threads and they should be stored in an airtight container in a dark place.

Satay sauce: This is made from crushed peanuts and is flavoured with soy sauce, chilli, shallot, sugar, vinegar and garlic. Available in Oriental, Asian and some large supermarkets.

Sesame oil: This strongly-flavoured oil is used as a seasoning and is made from roasted sesame seeds. Usually added at the end of cooking. It is available from Oriental food stores and some supermarkets.

Shrimp powder: This pungent ingredient is available from Oriental food stores and some supermarkets. It is made by pounding dried salted shrimp to a powder. Do not be put off by the odour as this disappears when cooked with other ingredients.

Soy sauce: This is a brown, salty liquid made from fermented soya beans, wheat, yeast, salt and sometimes sugar. The Chinese tend to use light soy sauce for cooking. Dark soy sauce is aged for longer than the light one, is slightly thicker and has a stronger flavour. The Chinese prefer to use this sauce as a dipping sauce and in stews.

Spring roll wrappers: Commercially prepared dough is available in Chinese supermarkets. It is rolled very thinly and cut into squares, but filo pastry can be used with equally good results.

Star anise: This is the star-shaped fruit of an Oriental evergreen of the magnolia family. When dried it is a brown colour and the flavour is one of pungent aniseed. Whole stars store well in an airtight container and are available from Oriental food stores and some supermarkets.

Straw mushrooms: These are mushrooms that are grown on beds of straw and they have a subtle taste and slippery texture. Available in cans, they should be thoroughly rinsed and drained after opening.

Tofu: Also known as bean curd, tofu has played an important role in Oriental cooking for over a thousand years. It is made from yellow soy beans which are soaked, ground and mixed with water then briefly cooked before being solidified. Rich in protein, it is low in fat and is cholesterol free. The range of bean curd products available in Oriental food stores is considerable and gives you an idea of how important this food is to the cuisines of the Far East.

Water chestnuts: White, crunchy and about the size of the walnut, water chestnuts are a sweet root vegetable. Canned water chestnuts are available from Oriental food stores and some supermarkets. In some Asian countries, fresh water chestnuts are boiled in their skins, then peeled and simmered with rock sugar and eaten as a snack. When using canned water chestnuts, rinse them well first.

White vinegar: This is sometimes called rice vinegar as

it is distilled from rice. Available from Chinese super-markets.

Wonton skins: These are made from flour, egg and water and are wafer thin wrappers for making small dumplings. They are sold fresh or frozen in Chinese supermarkets.

SERVING A MEAL

For a Chinese meal, all the dishes are served at once and placed in the centre of the table. Each person needs a soup bowl with a porcelain spoon, a slightly smaller bowl for rice with an underplate, and a pair of chopsticks.

It is difficult to give precise servings for Chinese dishes as they 'stretch' in a very accommodating way. As a rough guide you should allow one dish per person, plus a staple such as rice or noodles. So for four people you would serve four dishes, plus a rice and a soup. For more people, instead of increasing the quantity of ingredients, simply add more dishes so there is more variety. With a Chinese meal, the 'more the merrier'. A dessert dish is not compulsory, and a fruit salad or ice-cream will suffice.

Many of the recipes in this book can be incorporated into Western style meals – for instance, stir-fried vegetables go well with grilled or roast meat or fish and some of the chicken or meat dishes can be served with pasta, salads or potatoes.

So far as drinks are concerned, a Chinese meal can be accompanied by red, rosé, dry or sparkling white wine, light beer or lager or non-alcoholic drinks. At the end of the meal there is nothing more refreshing than the very fragrant Jasmine tea, served without milk or sugar.

USING CHOPSTICKS

1 Put the first chopstick in the hollow between your thumb and index finger and hold the lower end between the tops of your third and fourth fingers. This chopstick should stay rigid.

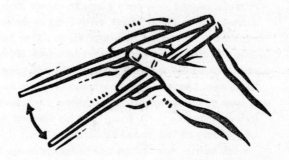

2 Hold the other chopstick as you would a pencil – between the tips of the index and middle fingers, steadying the upper part against the bottom of the index finger and use your thumb to keep it steady. This chopstick can be moved up and down, in a pincer movement.

SOUPS

Chinese soups are very easy to make and often consist of a clear broth with lots of delicious chunks of fish, meat or vegetables. The secret of a good soup is the stock that is used. Never use a stock cube as a short cut; it will not give a very 'Chinese' taste. If you can, make your own, or use one of the ready-made chilled varieties found in supermarkets. A soup can be served at the beginning of the meal or as a meal on its own with some rice as an accompaniment. The Chinese actually serve soup between courses and sometimes even at the end of a meal.

STOCK FOR SOUPS

REALLY EASY!

Chicken stock is the basis of many Chinese soups and for a more traditional flavour, you might like to make a Chinese chicken stock.

1 small chicken
2 carrots, roughly chopped
2 onions, roughly chopped
4 sticks celery, chopped
2.5 cm (1 inch) piece fresh ginger, peeled
2 teaspoons soy sauce

1 Cut chicken into pieces, place in a large saucepan. Add enough water to cover and bring to the boil. Reduce heat, cover and simmer for 1½ hours. Skim any fat from the surface as it rises.

2 Remove chicken from pan and use the cooked chicken for another recipe. Add vegetables and ginger to the pan, cover and simmer for 15 minutes.

3 Stir in soy sauce and simmer for 5 minutes longer. Strain stock, refrigerate, then remove fat from top of stock. Use at once or freeze until required.

ORIENTAL SEAFOOD SOUP

REALLY EASY!

A filling soup made with stock and chunky pieces of fish, ham, prawns, mushrooms, noodles and spinach.

Serves 4

4 large dried Chinese mushrooms
60g (2 oz) vermicelli noodles
1.5 litres (2½ pints) chicken stock
500g (1 lb) firm white fish fillets, cut into strips
60g (2 oz) ham, cut into strips
1 tablespoon soy sauce
250g (8 oz) cooked prawns, shelled and deveined
4 spring onions, chopped
4 large spinach leaves, shredded

1 Place mushrooms in a bowl and cover with boiling water. Set aside to soak for 20 minutes or until mushrooms are tender. Drain, remove stalks if necessary and chop mushrooms.

2 Cook noodles in boiling water in a large saucepan following packet directions. Drain and set aside.

3 Place stock in a large saucepan and bring to the boil. Reduce heat, add fish, ham and soy sauce and simmer for 2-3 minutes or until fish is just cooked. Stir in mushrooms, prawns, spring onions and spinach and cook for 2-3 minutes longer or until heated through.

4 To serve, place noodles in a large serving bowl, pour over soup and serve immediately.

BEEF AND TOMATO SOUP

REALLY EASY!

Thin strips of shredded beef, stir-fried and mixed with egg-thickened chicken stock and tomatoes.

Serves 4

125g (4 oz) fillet steak, thinly sliced and cut into strips
1 tablespoon dry sherry
2 teaspoons soy sauce
2 teaspoons cornflour
1 tablespoon oil
1.5 litres (2½ pints) chicken stock
2 tomatoes, peeled and chopped
2 eggs, beaten
2 spring onions, sliced

1 Place meat, sherry, soy sauce and cornflour in a bowl and mix to combine. Cover and set aside to stand at room temperature for 20 minutes.

2 Heat oil in a wok or large saucepan, add meat mixture and stir-fry for 2-3 minutes or until meat browns. Remove meat from pan and set aside.

3 Add stock and tomatoes to pan, bring to the boil and boil for 3-4 minutes or until tomatoes are just cooked. Stir beaten eggs into stock mixture.

4 Place meat in serving bowls, spoon over soup, sprinkle with spring onions and serve immediately.

ORIENTAL SEAFOOD SOUP • BEEF AND TOMATO SOUP

PRAWN AND WONTON SOUP

EASY!

Little parcels, containing spicy minced pork, in a clear soup with thin strips of vegetables and whole prawns.

Serves 6-8

2½ litres (4 pints) chicken stock
1 carrot, cut into thin strips
1 stick celery, cut into thin strips
½ red pepper, cut into thin strips
24 large cooked prawns, peeled and deveined

Pork Wontons

250g (8 oz) pork mince
1 egg, lightly beaten
2 spring onions, chopped
1 fresh red chilli, seeded and chopped
1 tablespoon soy sauce
1 tablespoon oyster sauce
24 spring roll or wonton wrappers, each 12.5cm
(5 inches) square

1 To make wontons, place pork, egg, spring onions, chilli, soy sauce and oyster sauce in a bowl and mix to combine.

2 Place teaspoonfuls of mixture in the centre of each spring roll or wonton wrapper, brush edges with water, then draw the corners together and twist to form small bundles. Place wontons in a steamer set over a saucepan of boiling water and steam for about 5 minutes or until wontons are cooked.

3 Place chicken stock in a saucepan and bring to the boil over a medium heat. Add carrot, celery and red pepper and simmer for 1 minute. Add prawns and cook for 1 minute longer.

4 To serve, place 3-4 wontons in each soup bowl and carefully ladle over the soup. Serve immediately.

GARLIC PORK SPARE RIB SOUP

E A S Y !

**A spicy stock containing tender pieces
of spare ribs.**

Serves 4

*1.5 kg (3 lb) pork spare ribs, separated and each cut in
half
1.5 litres (2½ pints) water
1 tablespoon dark soy sauce
90 ml (3 fl oz) light soy sauce
1 tablespoon muscovado or Demerara sugar
½ teaspoon salt
300g (10 oz) sliced Chinese fried bread sticks
(yau-char-kwai) (optional)
2 tablespoons chopped fresh coriander
2 red chillies, seeded and finely chopped*

Spice Bag
*10-12 cloves garlic, lightly bruised
4 whole cloves
2 star anise
1 tablespoon whole white or black peppercorns,
lightly crushed
1 piece muslin, 20 cm (8 inch) square*

1 Place ribs in a large saucepan and pour over enough hot water to cover. Bring to the boil over a medium heat and boil for 4-5 minutes. Remove from heat, drain ribs and rinse under cold running water to remove scum. Discard cooking water.

2 To make Spice Bag, place garlic, cloves, star anise and white or black peppercorns in the centre of the piece of muslin. Draw up corners and tie securely.

3 Place water and Spice Bag in a large saucepan and

bring to the boil. Add parboiled spare ribs, dark soy sauce, light soy sauce, sugar and salt, reduce heat, cover and simmer for about 1 hour or until ribs are tender. Garnish with bread slices, if using. Sprinkle with coriander and serve with chillies.

GARLIC PORK SPARE RIB SOUP

SEAFOOD AND TOFU SOUP

EASY!

A hearty soup with prawns, squid, white fish and tofu, flavoured with ginger, carrot, chicken stock and spring onions.

Serves 4

10 uncooked medium prawns, peeled and deveined, tails left intact
125g (4 oz) squid, cleaned
½ teaspoon salt
½ teaspoon sugar
½ teaspoon cornflour
¼ teaspoon freshly ground black pepper
¼ teaspoon sesame oil
water
180g (6 oz) firm white fish fillet, sliced
1 tablespoon vegetable oil
3-5 thin slices peeled fresh ginger
300g (10 oz) firm tofu, halved lengthwise and sliced
1 small carrot, sliced
1 teaspoon chicken stock powder
2-3 spring onions, cut into 2.5 cm (1 inch) lengths

1 Cut prawns in half lengthwise. Make a single cut down the length of each squid tube or body and open out. Using a sharp knife, cut parallel lines down the length of the squid, taking care not to cut right through the flesh. Make more cuts in the opposite direction to form a diamond pattern. Cut each one into 3 or 4 pieces.

2 Place salt, sugar, cornflour, black pepper, sesame oil and 1 tablespoon water in a bowl and mix to combine. Add prawns, squid and fish, toss to combine and set aside to marinate for 10-15 minutes.

3 Heat vegetable oil in a wok or large saucepan, add ginger and stir-fry for 2-3 minutes. Stir in 750 ml (1¼ pints) water and bring to the boil. Add seafood mixture, tofu, carrot and chicken stock powder and cook for 5 minutes or until seafood is cooked. Remove pan from heat, sprinkle with spring onions and serve immediately.

SEAFOOD AND TOFU SOUP

TOMATO AND EGG THREAD SOUP

REALLY EASY!

To achieve perfect 'threads' in soups and stocks, it is important to switch the heat off before adding the beaten egg mixture. If the eggs are added to soup while the heat is still on, lumpy and firm blobs will result rather than delicate threads.

Serves 2

1 tablespoon light soy sauce
½ teaspoon cornflour
2 tablespoons vegetable oil
½ teaspoon sesame oil
¼ teaspoon sugar
¼ teaspoon salt
125g (4 oz) lean pork mince
500 ml (16 fl oz) water
2 cloves garlic, lightly bruised
1 large tomato, skinned and cut into wedges
2 eggs, lightly beaten with ½ teaspoon salt and
¼ teaspoon sugar
1 tablespoon chopped fresh coriander

1 Place soy sauce, cornflour, 1 tablespoon vegetable oil, sesame oil, sugar and salt in a bowl and mix. Add pork, toss to combine and set aside to marinate for 10-15 minutes.

2 Place water, garlic and remaining vegetable oil in a saucepan and bring to the boil. Stir in pork mixture, bring to simmering and simmer for 3-5 minutes or until pork is cooked. Add tomato and simmer for 1 minute longer. Switch off heat and immediately stir egg mixture into soup – use a fork and circular motion so that the egg mixture forms thin threads in the soup. Sprinkle with coriander and serve immediately.

TOMATO AND EGG THREAD SOUP

CREAMY CORN AND CRAB SOUP

REALLY EASY!

A quickly made creamy soup with sweetcorn and crabmeat, thickened with cornflour and egg.

Serves 4
400g (14 oz) canned creamed sweetcorn
450 ml (15 fl oz) water
180g (6 oz) fresh crabmeat
1½ teaspoons cornflour blended with 1 tablespoon water
1 egg, lightly beaten
1 teaspoon vinegar
¼ teaspoon sugar
freshly ground black pepper

1 Place sweetcorn and water in a saucepan and bring to the boil over a medium heat. Stir in crabmeat and cornflour mixture and bring to simmering. Remove from heat, stir in egg, vinegar and sugar and season to taste with black pepper. Serve immediately.

35

FISH AND CORIANDER SOUP

REALLY EASY!

A soup delicately flavoured with ginger, soy sauce and coriander with moist flakes of white fish.

Serves 4

*250g (8 oz) firm white fish fillets, cut into 2.5 cm
(1 inch) pieces
1 tablespoon cornflour
1 litre (1¾ pints) chicken stock
2 teaspoons grated fresh ginger
2 teaspoons soy sauce
2 tablespoons cider vinegar
2 tablespoons chopped fresh coriander*

1 Toss fish pieces in cornflour and set aside.

2 Place stock, ginger, soy sauce and vinegar in a large saucepan and bring to the boil. Reduce heat, add fish and simmer for 2-3 minutes or until fish is just cooked. Stir in coriander and serve immediately.

STARTERS

Most chinese families would eat many of the
following dishes as part of a single course, but in
the West we tend to eat these little treats as a
starter or appetiser. They make good snacks or
light meals and although they appear to be fiddly
they are surprisingly easy to create.

SPRING ROLLS

E A S Y !

Finely chopped pork, bean sprouts and cabbage, encased in a spring roll wrapper and deep-fried until crisp.

Makes 12

12 spring roll or wonton wrappers, each 12.5 cm
(5 inches) square
vegetable oil for deep-frying

Pork And Vegetable Filling
125g (4 oz) lean pork mince
30g (1 oz) bean sprouts
¼ small cabbage, chopped
2 spring onions, chopped
1 tablespoon cornflour
1 tablespoon soy sauce
1 teaspoon sesame oil

1 To make filling, place pork, bean sprouts, cabbage, spring onions, cornflour, soy sauce and sesame oil in a bowl and mix to combine.

2 Place a tablespoon of filling in the centre of each wrapper, fold one corner over filling, then tuck in the sides and roll up, sealing with water.

3 Heat vegetable oil in a large saucepan until a cube of bread, when dropped in, browns in 50 seconds. Cook a few Spring Rolls at a time for 3-4 minutes or until golden. Drain on absorbent kitchen paper and serve immediately.

SAN CHOY BOW

REALLY EASY !

Minced pork with chillies, garlic, ginger and water chestnuts served in lettuce leaves and eaten with your fingers. You might like to serve these as they do in restaurants. Serve the meat and lettuce leaves separately and allow each person to assemble their own, so preventing the lettuce from becoming soggy.

Makes 12
1 tablespoon vegetable oil
500g (1 lb) lean pork mince
1 tablespoon cornflour
180 ml (6 fl oz) water
1 tablespoon dry sherry
½ teaspoon sesame oil
1 tablespoon oyster sauce
2 small fresh red chillies, chopped
1 clove garlic, crushed
1 teaspoon grated fresh ginger
200g (7 oz) canned water chestnuts, drained and chopped
12 small 'cupped' lettuce leaves

1 Heat oil in a large wok or frying pan, add mince and stir-fry for 4-5 minutes or until browned. Remove from pan and drain on absorbent kitchen paper. Wipe pan clean.

2 Place cornflour, water, sherry, sesame oil and oyster sauce in a bowl, mix to combine and set aside. Return mince to pan, add chillies, garlic, ginger, water chestnuts and cornflour mixture and cook over a high heat, stirring constantly, for 4-5 minutes or until mixture boils and thickens and pork is cooked.

3 Spoon hot pork mixture into lettuce leaves and serve immediately.

STEAMED PORK WONTONS

EASY!

**Little steamed dumplings filled with pork,
mushrooms, bamboo shoots and celery.**

Makes 36
2 dried Chinese mushrooms
180g (6 oz) lean pork mince
1 tablespoon chopped canned bamboo shoots
2 tablespoons finely chopped celery
1 spring onion, finely chopped
1 clove garlic, crushed
1 tablespoon soy sauce
1 tablespoon dry sherry
1 teaspoon sugar
36 wonton or spring roll wrappers, each 12.5 cm
(5 inches) square

1 Place mushrooms in a bowl, cover with boiling water and set aside to soak for 20 minutes or until mushrooms are tender. Drain, remove stalks if necessary and chop mushrooms.

2 Place mushrooms, pork, bamboo shoots, celery, spring onion, garlic, soy sauce, sherry and sugar in a bowl and mix well to combine. Cover and refrigerate for 30 minutes or until ready to cook wontons.

3 Place a teaspoon of pork mixture in the centre of each wrapper, brush edges with water, draw wrapper up around mixture and pinch together. Place wontons in a bamboo steamer set over a saucepan of simmering water, cover and cook for 10 minutes or until wontons are cooked through.

SAN CHOY BOW • STEAMED PORK WONTONS

EGG ROLLS

**Egg pancakes filled with prawns, pork, leeks,
bean sprouts, celery and seasonings and
then deep-fried.**

Makes 8-12 depending on size of pancakes

Prawn And Pork Filling
1 tablespoon peanut (groundnut) oil
*125g (4 oz) uncooked prawns, peeled, deveined and
chopped*
180g (6 oz) lean pork mince
2 small leeks, cut into thin strips
60g (2 oz) bean sprouts
1 tablespoon finely chopped celery
1 clove garlic
1 tablespoon soy sauce
2-3 drops Tabasco sauce

Pancakes
250g (8 oz) flour
4 eggs
180 ml (6 fl oz) water

vegetable oil for deep-frying

1 To make filling, heat peanut (groundnut) oil in a large
wok or frying pan, add prawns, pork, leeks, bean sprouts,
celery and garlic and stir-fry for 3 minutes. Add soy and
Tabasco sauces and simmer, stirring frequently, for 10
minutes. Remove meat mixture from pan and set aside.

2 To make pancakes, place flour, eggs and water in a
bowl and beat until smooth. Pour 2-3 tablespoons batter
into a lightly greased frying pan and cook over a medium
heat for 3-4 minutes or until top of pancake is dry. Slide

cooked pancake onto a plate. Repeat with remaining mixture to make 8-12 pancakes.

3 Place a spoonful of filling in the centre of each pancake, brush edges with water, fold in the sides and gently roll up to form a parcel.

4 Heat oil in a large wok or frying pan until a cube of bread, when dropped in, browns in 50 seconds. Cook 3-4 parcels at a time for 5-7 minutes or until golden and crisp and heated through. Drain on kitchen paper. Cut each roll into three and serve immediately.

SESAME PRAWN BALLS

REALLY EASY!

**Tiny balls made with chopped prawns, ground
rice and spices, coated in sesame seeds
and deep-fried.**

Serves 6

1 kg (2 lb) uncooked prawns, peeled and deveined
1 onion, chopped
½ teaspoon five spice powder
180g (6 oz) ground rice
1 teaspoon sesame oil
2 tablespoons finely chopped fresh coriander
3 tablespoons sesame seeds
vegetable oil for deep-frying

1 Place prawns, onion and five spice powder in a food processor and process until smooth. Transfer prawn mixture to a bowl, add ground rice, sesame oil and coriander and mix well to combine. Cover and refrigerate for at least 1 hour.

2 Using wet hands, roll mixture into small balls, then roll in sesame seeds. Place balls on a plate lined with plastic food wrap and refrigerate for 30 minutes.

3 Heat oil in a large wok or saucepan until a cube of bread, when dropped in, browns in 50 seconds. Cook 5-6 balls at a time for 4-5 minutes or until golden and heated through. Drain on absorbent kitchen paper and serve immediately.

SESAME PRAWN TOASTS

EASY!

Crisp fingers of bread topped with minced prawns and sesame seeds.

Serves 4

180g (6 oz) uncooked prawns, peeled and deveined
1 teaspoon grated fresh ginger
1 clove garlic, crushed
2 teaspoons cornflour
1 egg white
⅛ teaspoon five spice powder
freshly ground black pepper
4 thin slices white bread, crusts removed
3 tablespoons sesame seeds
vegetable oil for shallow-frying

1 Place prawns, ginger, garlic and cornflour in a food processor and process to mince prawns.

2 Place egg white in a bowl and whisk with a fork until frothy. Stir egg white into prawn mixture. Add five spice powder and season to taste with black pepper.

3 Press prawn mixture evenly and firmly onto bread slices. Sprinkle with sesame seeds and press firmly. Heat 2 cm (¾ inch) oil in a large frying pan. Place prawn-covered bread, prawn side down in hot oil and fry for 2-3 minutes or until golden. To keep bread slices immersed during cooking, hold down with a fish slice. Remove prawn toasts from oil, drain on absorbent kitchen paper, cut into fingers and serve immediately.

PORK BALLS WITH CHILLI SAUCE

EASY!

This is an excellent party starter. Serve pork balls on a platter with small bowls of the Chilli Dipping Sauce, or plum sauce for those guests who prefer to dip into something less spicy.

Makes 12
1 clove garlic, finely chopped
½ teaspoon salt
½ teaspoon sugar
½ teaspoon freshly ground black pepper
1 teaspoon cornflour
180g (6 oz) pork mince
1 tablespoon vegetable oil
30g (1 oz) dried breadcrumbs
vegetable oil for deep-frying
400g (14 oz) canned pineapple pieces, drained
3 spring onions, cut into 5 cm (2 inch) pieces

Chilli Dipping Sauce
90 ml (3 fl oz) chilli sauce
2 tablespoons tomato sauce
1 teaspoon sugar
½ teaspoon salt
½ teaspoon sesame oil
2 teaspoons sesame seeds

1 Place garlic, salt, sugar, black pepper and cornflour in a bowl and mix to combine. Add pork, toss in the mixture and set aside to marinate for 10-15 minutes.

2 To make dipping sauce, place chilli sauce, tomato sauce, sugar, salt, sesame oil and sesame seeds in a small bowl and mix well. Set aside.

3 Stir 1 tablespoon vegetable oil into pork mixture and mix to combine. Roll pork mixture into walnut-sized balls. Place a few pork balls at a time with the breadcrumbs in a plastic food bag and shake to coat balls with crumbs.

4 Heat vegetable oil in a wok or large saucepan until a cube of bread dropped in browns in 50 seconds. Cook pork balls, a few at a time, for 7-10 minutes or until golden and cooked through. Remove pork balls and drain on absorbent kitchen paper. Spear each pork ball with a toothpick or cocktail stick and serve with pineapple pieces, spring onions and dipping sauce.

PORK BALLS WITH CHILLI SAUCE

SAVOURY PANCAKES

Pancakes filled with a mixture of mushrooms, chicken, carrot, potato and fresh coriander.

Makes 8

Pancakes
125g (4 oz) flour
¼ teaspoon salt
pinch sugar
250 ml (8 fl oz) water
1 egg
1 teaspoon vegetable oil

Chicken And Vegetable Filling
3 dried Chinese mushrooms
1 tablespoon vegetable oil
1 small onion, diced
125g (4 oz) uncooked minced chicken
1 small carrot, diced
1 teaspoon light soy sauce
½ teaspoon salt
½ teaspoon sesame oil
½ teaspoon sugar
pinch freshly ground black pepper
2 large potatoes, cooked and mashed
2 tablespoons chopped fresh coriander

1 To make pancakes, place flour, salt and sugar in a bowl and mix to combine. Whisk in water, egg, and vegetable oil and continue to whisk until smooth.

2 Heat a lightly greased wok or frying pan over a high heat, pour 2 tablespoons batter into the pan and swirl pan so the batter covers the base thinly and evenly. Cook for 1-2 minutes or until bubbles form on the surface, then turn and cook for 1-2 minutes longer or until pancake is golden. Remove pancake from pan, set aside and keep warm. Repeat with remaining batter.

3 To make filling, place mushrooms in a bowl, cover with boiling water and set aside to soak for 20 minutes or until mushrooms are tender. Drain, remove stalks if necessary and dice mushrooms.

4 Heat vegetable oil in a wok or frying pan over a medium heat, add onion and stir-fry for 2-3 minutes or until onion is transparent. Add chicken and stir-fry for 2-3 minutes longer or until it changes colour. Stir in carrot, mushrooms, soy sauce, salt, sesame oil, sugar and black pepper and cook for 4-5 minutes longer or until carrot is soft. Add mashed potato and coriander and mix to combine. Remove pan from heat and set aside to cool.

5 Divide chicken mixture between pancakes and place in the centre of each one, fold in sides and roll up. Serve hot or warm.

CHINESE PORK BUNS

A spicy barbecue flavour pork filling encased in a light dough which is then steamed.

Makes 20
20 x 5 cm (2 inch) square pieces non-stick baking paper

Barbecued Pork Filling
1 tablespoon vegetable oil
180g (6 oz) Chinese barbecued pork or Chinese roast pork, diced
1 clove garlic, crushed
1 tablespoon oyster sauce
1 teaspoon light soy sauce
½ teaspoon sesame oil
¾ teaspoon sugar
¼ teaspoon salt
¼ teaspoon freshly ground black pepper
1 tablespoon cornflour blended with 5 tablespoons water
2 tablespoons chopped fresh coriander

Bun Dough
250g (8 oz) self-raising flour
1 tablespoon baking powder
90g (3 oz) sugar
180 ml (6 fl oz) water

1 To make the filling, heat vegetable oil in a wok or frying pan over a medium heat, add pork and garlic and stir-fry for 2-3 minutes. Stir in oyster sauce, soy sauce, sesame oil, sugar, salt, black pepper and cornflour mixture and bring to a gentle boil. Simmer for 3-4 minutes or until mixture is quite dry. Remove pan from heat, stir in coriander and set aside to cool completely.

2 To make dough, sift flour and baking powder together

into a large bowl. Add sugar and mix to combine. Mix in enough water to form a soft dough. Turn dough onto a lightly floured surface and knead for 10 minutes or until the dough is smooth. Cover and set aside to rest for 30 minutes.

3 Divide dough into 20 portions and working on a lightly floured surface, roll each portion into a ball. Lightly flatten each ball of dough to make a 7.5 cm (3 inch) round. Place a teaspoon of filling in the centre of each dough round and brush the edges with water. Draw pastry around mixture and pinch together to form a bun.

4 Place bun, join side up, on a piece of the non-stick baking paper and place in a bamboo steamer. Repeat with remaining dough rounds to use all ingredients.

5 Cover the steamer with a lid, place over a saucepan of simmering water and steam for 10-15 minutes or until buns are cooked through.

GARLIC PORK ROLLS

EASY!

Bean curd sheets wrapped around a filling of pork, water chestnuts, onion, garlic and spices, and then deep-fried. Serve with a salad of sliced cucumber, sliced tomatoes and pineapple pieces and accompany with chilli sauce for dipping.

Makes 20

1 kg (2 lb) lean pork mince
350g (11 oz) canned water chestnuts, finely chopped
1 small onion, finely chopped
1 head garlic, cloves separated and crushed
2 egg whites, lightly beaten
90 ml (3 fl oz) vegetable oil
5 teaspoons muscovado or Demerara sugar
3½ teaspoons five spice powder
1½ teaspoons ground coriander
1 teaspoon salt
½ teaspoon freshly ground black pepper
2 teaspoons sesame oil
2 teaspoons light soy sauce
100g (3½ oz) dried bean curd sheets
vegetable oil for deep-frying

1 Place pork, water chestnuts, onion, garlic, half egg white mixture, vegetable oil, sugar, five spice powder, coriander, salt, black pepper, sesame oil and soy sauce in a bowl and mix to combine.

2 Cut bean curd sheet according to fold lines and wipe with a damp cloth. Place pork mixture along centre of bean curd sheets, fold in sides and roll up. Brush edges with remaining egg white and seal, cover and refrigerate overnight.

3 Heat vegetable oil in a wok or large saucepan until a

cube of bread, when dropped in, browns in 50 seconds. Cook rolls in batches, turning occasionally, for 5-10 minutes or until golden and cooked through. Remove rolls from pan and drain on absorbent kitchen paper. Slice and serve immediately.

GARLIC PORK ROLLS

FRIED PORK BALLS

E A S Y !

**Lightly spiced deep-fried mini pork balls.
Ideal as an appetiser.**

Makes 24
*500g (1 lb) lean pork mince
30g (1 oz) rice noodles, broken, soaked and well-drained
1 small onion, finely chopped
1 clove garlic, crushed
1 teaspoon grated fresh ginger
1 teaspoon finely chopped fresh lemon grass or
1 teaspoon finely grated lemon rind
¼ teaspoon ground turmeric
freshly ground black pepper
flour
vegetable oil for deep-frying*

1 Place pork and noodles in a bowl and mix to combine.

2 Place onion, garlic, ginger and lemon grass or lemon rind in a food processor or blender and process to make a paste. Add onion mixture, turmeric and black pepper to taste to meat mixture and mix well to combine.

3 Form meat mixture into 24 balls, dust with flour, place on a plate lined with plastic food wrap, cover and refrigerate until required. Heat oil in a large wok or saucepan until a cube of bread, when dropped in, browns in 50 seconds. Cook balls a few at a time for 3-4 minutes or until golden and cooked through. Drain on absorbent kitchen paper and serve immediately.

35

DEEP-FRIED WONTONS

REALLY EASY!

Little dumplings filled with pork and spinach and then deep-fried until crisp.

Makes 36

250g (8 oz) lean pork mince
2 teaspoons soy sauce
180g (6 oz) frozen spinach, thawed and excess water squeezed out
freshly ground black pepper
36 wonton or spring roll wrappers, each 12.5 cm (5 inch) square
vegetable oil for deep-frying

1 Place pork, soy sauce, spinach and black pepper to taste in a bowl and mix well to combine.

2 Place a teaspoon of pork mixture in the centre of each wrapper, brush edges with water, draw wrapper up around mixture and pinch together.

3 Heat oil in a large wok or saucepan until a cube of bread, when dropped in, browns in 50 seconds. Cook wontons a few at a time for 3-4 minutes or until golden and cooked through. Drain on absorbent kitchen paper and serve immediately.

FRIED PORK BALLS • DEEP-FRIED WONTONS

PRAWN AND PORK TOAST

REALLY EASY!

Crisp deep-fried triangles of bread topped with prawns, pork and sesame seeds.

Serves 4

4 medium uncooked prawns, peeled and deveined, finely chopped
125g (4 oz) pork mince
1 small onion, finely chopped
¾ teaspoon salt
¼ teaspoon freshly ground black pepper
¼ teaspoon sesame oil
4 slices wholemeal bread, crusts trimmed
2 tablespoons sesame seeds
vegetable oil for deep-frying
chilli sauce

1 Place prawns, pork, onion, salt, black pepper and sesame oil in a bowl and mix to combine. Set aside to marinate for 10-15 minutes.

2 Spread each bread slice with pork mixture and sprinkle with sesame seeds. Cut each slice into 4 triangles.

3 Heat vegetable oil in a wok or large saucepan until a cube of bread, when dropped in, browns in 50 seconds. Cook triangles of pork side down, a few at a time, for 4-5 minutes or until golden and cooked through. Remove and drain on absorbent kitchen paper. Serve immediately with chilli sauce for dipping.

WAFER-WRAPPED PRAWNS

EASY!

**Chopped prawns inside crispy wonton wrappers
served with Chilli Sauce.**

Makes 24

*350g (12 oz) cooked prawns, peeled, deveined and
coarsely chopped
1 fresh green chilli, seeded and chopped
2 teaspoons oyster sauce
24 spring roll or wonton wrappers each 12.5 cm (5 inch)
square
vegetable oil for deep-frying*

Chilli Sauce

*4 tablespoons tomato sauce
1-2 teaspoons chilli sauce
water
½ teaspoon sesame oil*

1 Place prawns, green chilli and oyster sauce in a bowl and mix well to combine.

2 Place a heaped teaspoon of prawn mixture in the centre of each wrapper, then draw the corners together and twist them to form small bundles.

3 To make sauce, place tomato sauce, chilli sauce, water and sesame oil in a small saucepan. Cook over a medium heat, stirring constantly for 1-2 minutes or until heated through.

4 Heat vegetable oil in a large saucepan until a cube of bread, when dropped in, browns in 50 seconds. Cook a few bundles at a time for 3-4 minutes or until golden. Drain on kitchen paper. Serve immediately with chilli sauce.

PRAWN AND PORK TOAST • WAFER-WRAPPED PRAWNS

FISH AND SEAFOOD

China has an abundance of rivers and a large
coastline and so the Chinese eat large amounts
of seafood and freshwater fish. Unfortunately, in
restaurants here, we often only see dishes with
prawns, such as Chow Mein. Fish lends itself
well to quick cooking methods such as stir-frying
and you will find in this chapter some delicious
ways of cooking fish, crab, squid, clams
and of course prawns.

PRAWN FOO YUNG

REALLY EASY!

This dish is also delicious made with crab meat or fish, or you might like to try a vegetarian version using asparagus and mangetout.

Serves 2

500g (1 lb) uncooked prawns, peeled and deveined
1 egg white, lightly beaten
1 teaspoon cornflour
2 eggs
1 teaspoon sesame oil
60 ml (2 fl oz) chicken stock
2 teaspoons dry sherry
2 teaspoons soy sauce
2 tablespoons vegetable oil
3 spring onions, finely chopped

1 Place prawns, egg white and cornflour in a bowl and mix to combine. Cover and refrigerate for 20 minutes.

2 Place eggs, sesame oil, stock, sherry and soy sauce in a bowl and whisk to combine.

3 Heat 1 tablespoon vegetable oil in a wok or frying pan, add prawns and stir-fry for 2-3 minutes or until prawns just change colour. Remove prawns from pan and set aside. Wipe pan clean.

4 Heat remaining oil in pan, add egg mixture and stir-fry for 1 minute or until egg just begins to set. Return prawns to pan and stir-fry for 1 minute longer. Sprinkle with spring onions and serve immediately.

FISH IN CHILLI BEAN SAUCE

REALLY EASY!

Strips of fish quickly stir-fried and served in a yellow bean sauce with a hint of chilli.

Serves 4

*500g (1 lb) firm white fish fillets, cut into 5 cm (2 inch)
wide strips*
3 tablespoons cornflour
peanut (groundnut) oil
*2 spring onions, sliced diagonally into 5 cm (2 inch)
lengths*
1 clove garlic, finely chopped
1 teaspoon finely chopped fresh ginger

Chilli Bean Sauce

60 ml (2 fl oz) chicken stock
2 teaspoons yellow bean sauce
¼ teaspoon chilli powder or to taste
1 tablespoon dry sherry
2 teaspoons soy sauce
1 teaspoon sesame oil

1 Toss fish strips in cornflour and set aside.

2 To make sauce, place stock, bean sauce, chilli powder, sherry, soy sauce and sesame oil in a small bowl and mix to combine. Set aside.

3 Heat peanut (groundnut) oil in a wok or large frying pan, add fish and stir-fry for 4-5 minutes or until golden and cooked through. Remove fish from pan, drain on absorbent kitchen paper and set aside.

4 Drain all but 1 tablespoon oil from pan, add spring onions, garlic and ginger and stir-fry for 30 seconds. Add sauce and bring to the boil. Reduce heat, return fish to pan and cook, stirring frequently, for 2 minutes or until heated through. Serve immediately.

SEAFOOD COMBINATION

REALLY EASY!

A wonderful stir-fry of prawns, squid, white fish, scallops, red pepper, mangetout and bamboo shoots.

Serves 4
60 ml (2 fl oz) vegetable oil
350g (12 oz) uncooked large prawns, peeled and deveined
250g (8 oz) squid, rings
250g (8 oz) firm white fish fillets, cut into cubes
125g (4 oz) prepared scallops
1 red pepper, cut into strips
250g (8 oz) mangetout
200g (7 oz) canned sliced bamboo shoots, drained
2 cloves garlic, crushed
2 teaspoons grated fresh ginger
2 teaspoons cornflour
125 ml (4 fl oz) chicken stock
1 teaspoon sesame oil
2 teaspoons soy sauce

1 Heat 2 tablespoons vegetable oil in a wok or frying pan, add prawns, squid, fish and scallops and stir-fry for 2-3 minutes. Remove seafood from pan and set aside.

2 Add remaining vegetable oil to pan, heat and add red pepper, mangetout, bamboo shoots, garlic and ginger and stir-fry for 4-5 minutes or until red pepper and mangetout are tender.

3 Combine cornflour, chicken stock, sesame oil and soy sauce and stir into pan. Cook, stirring constantly, until sauce boils and thickens. Return seafood to pan and cook for 2-3 minutes or until heated through. Serve immediately.

STEAMED FISH

REALLY EASY!

Whole fish marinated in ginger, soy sauce, sugar and vinegar and then steamed until moist and tender. The Chinese always serve whole fish with the head pointing towards the guest of honour. It is believed that this assures him or her of good fortune.

Serves 2

2 small whole fish, such as snapper, bream, trout or mackerel
1 tablespoon finely chopped fresh ginger
1 tablespoon soy sauce
1 teaspoon sugar
1 tablespoon white vinegar
2 rashers bacon, cut into strips
1 small carrot, cut into thin strips
4 spring onions, cut into 3 cm (1¼ inch) lengths

1 Place fish in a shallow glass or ceramic dish. Combine ginger, soy sauce, sugar and vinegar. Pour soy mixture over fish, cover and set aside to marinate for 30 minutes.

2 Line a large bamboo steamer with greaseproof or non-stick baking paper. Place fish in steamer, pour over marinade and sprinkle with bacon, carrot and spring onions.

3 Cover steamer, place over a wok of simmering water and steam for 10-15 minutes or until fish flakes when tested with a fork.

SEAFOOD AND NOODLE STIR-FRY

Cooked noodles with asparagus, chillies and mixed seafood, moistened with a Tomato Sauce.

Serves 4
350g (12 oz) egg noodles
250g (8 oz) squid hoods (body tubes)
250g (8 oz) asparagus, cut diagonally into 5 cm (2 inch) pieces
2 tablespoons peanut (groundnut) oil
1 clove garlic, crushed
2 small fresh red chillies, finely chopped
1 teaspoon finely grated fresh ginger
500g (1 lb) uncooked large prawns, peeled and deveined, tails left intact
250g (8 oz) prepared scallops
½ red pepper, sliced
60g (2 oz) mangetout, sliced diagonally into 5 cm (2 inch) pieces
2 tablespoons sesame seeds, toasted

Tomato Sauce
1 tablespoon cornflour
1 tablespoon sugar
3 tablespoons tomato sauce
1 teaspoon oyster sauce
1 tablespoon soy sauce
1 teaspoon sesame oil
250 ml (8 fl oz) water

1 Cook noodles in a large saucepan of boiling water following packet instructions. Drain, then rinse under hot water. Spread out on absorbent kitchen paper.

2 Cut squid hoods along one side and spread out flat with inside facing up, Using a sharp knife mark a diamond pattern over the surface, then cut into diamond-shaped pieces. Set aside.

3 Boil, steam or microwave asparagus until it just changes colour. Drain and rinse under cold running water. Set aside.

4 Heat peanut (groundnut) oil in a wok or frying pan, add garlic, chillies and ginger and stir-fry for 1 minute. Add squid, prawns, scallops, red pepper, mangetout and asparagus and stir-fry for 2-3 minutes or until prawns just change colour. Add noodles to pan and stir-fry for 1-2 minutes longer.

5 To make sauce, place cornflour, sugar, tomato sauce, oyster sauce, soy sauce, sesame oil and water in a small bowl and whisk to combine. Pour sauce into pan and heat for 2-3 minutes longer or until it boils and thickens. Sprinkle with sesame seeds and serve immediately.

SEAFOOD AND NOODLE STIR-FRY

PRAWN CHOW MEIN

EASY!

Chow Mein means 'stir-fried' noodles. In this recipe the main ingredient is prawns but Chow Mein can be made with almost anything that you like. Left over Chow Mein is delicious served cold as a salad.

Serves 4
250g (8 oz) dried egg noodles
1 kg (2 lb) uncooked prawns, peeled, deveined and roughly chopped
2 teaspoons dry sherry
1 tablespoon soy sauce
1 tablespoon peanut (groundnut) oil
1 clove garlic, crushed
60g (2 oz) mangetout
2 rashers bacon, chopped
½ teaspoon sugar
2 spring onions, chopped
1 teaspoon sesame oil

1 Cook noodles in boiling water in a large saucepan following packet directions. Drain and place in cold water until ready to use.

2 Place prawns, sherry and 2 teaspoons soy sauce in a bowl and toss to combine. Cover and set aside to marinate for 15 minutes.

3 Heat 2 teaspoons peanut (groundnut) oil in a wok or large frying pan, add prawns and stir-fry for 2 minutes or until prawns just change colour. Remove prawns from pan and set aside. Wipe pan clean.

4 Drain noodles, place on absorbent kitchen paper and pat dry. Heat remaining peanut (groundnut) oil in pan, add garlic, mangetout and bacon and stir-fry for 2-3 minutes or until mangetout just change colour and bacon is cooked. Add noodles, sugar, spring onions and remaining soy sauce and stir-fry for 2 minutes, then add prawns and stir-fry for 2 minutes longer or until heated through. Stir in sesame oil and serve immediately.

PRAWN CHOW MEIN

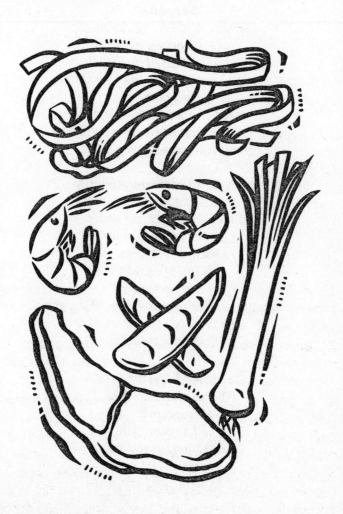

STUFFED BABY SQUID

Small squid hoods (body tube) stuffed with a pork and mushroom filling and cooked in Garlic and Oyster Sauce.

Serves 4
16 baby squid hoods, cleaned
1 tablespoon vegetable oil
60g (2 oz) canned sweetcorn, drained
60g (2 oz) fresh or frozen peas
¼ teaspoon salt
2 fresh red chillies, seeded and sliced
2 tablespoons chopped fresh coriander
freshly ground black pepper

Pork And Mushroom Filling
4 dried Chinese mushrooms
1 teaspoon light soy sauce
½ teaspoon cornflour
½ teaspoon sesame oil
¼ teaspoon salt
¼ teaspoon sugar
¼ teaspoon freshly ground black pepper
125g (4 oz) pork mince
2 tablespoons grated carrot

Garlic And Oyster Sauce
1 teaspoon cornflour
½ teaspoon sugar
½ teaspoon salt
2 teaspoons oyster sauce
4 tablespoons water
2 cloves garlic, crushed

1 To make filling, place mushrooms in a bowl, cover

with boiling water and set aside to soak for 20 minutes or until mushrooms are tender. Drain, remove stalks if necessary and cut mushrooms in half.

2 Place soy sauce, cornflour, sesame oil, salt, sugar and black pepper in a bowl and mix to combine. Add pork, carrot and mushrooms, toss together and set aside to marinate for 10-15 minutes.

3 To make sauce, place cornflour, sugar, salt, oyster sauce, water and garlic in a small bowl and mix to combine. Set aside.

4 Rinse squid under cold running water and pat dry with absorbent kitchen paper. Three-quarters fill each squid hood with filling and secure opening with a wooden toothpick or cocktail stick.

5 Heat vegetable oil in wok or frying pan over a medium heat, add stuffed squid and stir-fry for 5-6 minutes or until filling expands. Add sweetcorn, peas and salt to pan and stir-fry for 3-4 minutes longer. Add sauce, bring to simmering and remove pan from heat. Sprinkle with chillies, coriander and black pepper to taste and serve immediately.

STUFFED BABY SQUID

HOT AND TANGY PRAWNS

REALLY EASY!

Prawns stir-fried with ginger, chillies, garlic and spring onions and served in a Tomato Chilli Sauce.

Serves 4
½ teaspoon salt
½ teaspoon sugar
¼ teaspoon freshly ground black pepper
20 medium uncooked prawns, peeled and deveined, tails left intact
2 tablespoons vegetable oil
6 thin slices peeled fresh ginger
4 cloves garlic, thinly sliced
3 fresh red chillies, sliced
2 spring onions, cut into 5 cm (2 inch) lengths
1 tomato, cut into wedges
1 onion, cut into wedges
1 lettuce, leaves separated

Tomato Chilli Sauce
180 ml (6 fl oz) tomato ketchup or sauce
1½ tablespoons chilli sauce
1 teaspoon sugar
½ teaspoon salt
1½ teaspoons light soy sauce

1 Place salt, sugar and black pepper in a bowl and mix to combine. Add prawns, toss to coat and set aside to marinate for 10-15 minutes.

2 To make sauce, place tomato ketchup or sauce, chilli sauce, sugar, salt and soy sauce in a bowl and mix to combine. Set aside.

3 Heat vegetable oil in wok or frying pan over a medium

heat, add ginger, garlic, chillies, spring onions and prawn mixture and stir-fry for 3-4 minutes or until prawns change colour.

4 Add sauce to pan and stir-fry for 1-2 minutes or until heated through. Add tomato and onion and stir-fry for 2-3 minutes longer. Line a serving platter with lettuce leaves, top with prawn mixture and serve immediately.

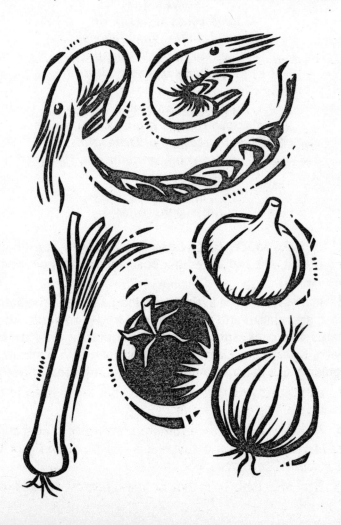

CLAMS IN BLACK BEAN SAUCE

REALLY EASY!

Clams in their shells quickly stir-fried with a Black Bean Sauce.

Serves 4
2 tablespoons vegetable oil
5 fresh red chillies, finely chopped
4 cloves garlic, finely chopped
1 kg (2 lb) clams in shells, cleaned

Black Bean Sauce
1½ tablespoons black bean garlic sauce
¾ teaspoon muscovado or Demerara sugar
½ teaspoon cornflour
¼ teaspoon sesame oil
pinch salt
2 teaspoons water

1 To make sauce, place bean sauce, sugar, cornflour, sesame oil, salt and water in a bowl and mix to combine. Set aside.

2 Heat vegetable oil in wok or frying pan over a medium heat, add chillies and garlic and stir-fry 1-2 minutes. Add clams and cook, stirring, for 4-5 minutes or until shells open. Discard any clams that do not open after 5 minutes cooking. Stir in sauce and cook for 1-2 minutes longer.

STIR-FRIED SQUID

REALLY EASY!

Squid quickly stir-fried with garlic, chillies, onion and ginger.

Serves 4

500g (1 lb) squid, cleaned
3 tablespoons vegetable oil
4 cloves garlic, sliced
4 fresh red chillies, sliced
5 cm (2 inch) piece fresh ginger, peeled and sliced
1 small onion, sliced
1½ teaspoons cornflour blended with 4 tablespoons water
1½ teaspoons light soy sauce
1 teaspoon lemon juice
½ teaspoon salt
½ teaspoon sugar
½ teaspoon sesame oil
3 spring onions, cut into 3 cm (1¼ inch) lengths

1 Using a sharp knife cut down the length of each squid tube or body and lay out flat. Cut parallel lines down the length of squid, taking care not to cut right through the flesh. Make more cuts in the opposite direction to form a diamond pattern. Cut each piece into 3 or 4 pieces.

2 Heat vegetable oil in wok or frying pan over a high heat, add garlic, chillies, ginger, onion and squid pieces and stir-fry for 1-2 minutes or until squid is opaque. Add cornflour mixture, soy sauce, lemon juice, salt, sugar, sesame oil and spring onions and stir-fry for 1-2 minutes longer. Serve immediately.

STIR-FRIED FISH AND VEGETABLES

EASY!

Fish fillets stir-fried with sweetcorn, carrots and spring onions and moistened with a Sherry Sauce.

Serves 4

350g (12 oz) boneless fish fillet, such as cod, plaice etc
½ teaspoon salt
½ teaspoon cornflour
¼ teaspoon sugar
¼ teaspoon freshly ground black pepper
½ teaspoon water
2 ½ tablespoons vegetable oil
6-8 thin slices peeled fresh ginger
5 cobs canned or fresh cooked baby sweet corn, drained and cut in half lengthwise then crosswise
½ carrot, sliced
2 spring onions, cut into 2.5 cm (1 inch) lengths

Sherry Sauce

180 ml (6 fl oz) water
¾ teaspoon cornflour
1 teaspoon salt
½ teaspoon muscovado or Demerara sugar
½ teaspoon sesame oil
½ teaspoon light soy sauce
½ teaspoon sweet sherry

1 Pat fish fillets dry with absorbent kitchen paper and set aside. Place salt, cornflour, sugar, black pepper and water in a bowl and mix to combine. Add fish fillets, toss to coat and set aside to marinate for 10-15 minutes.

2 To make sauce, combine water, cornflour, salt, sugar,

sesame oil, soy sauce and sherry in a bowl. Set aside.

3 Heat 2 tablespoons vegetable oil in wok or frying pan over a medium heat, add ginger and stir-fry for 1-2 minutes. Add fish fillets and stir-fry for 2-3 minutes or until almost cooked, add sweet corn and carrot, and stir-fry for 1-2 minutes longer. Remove fish and vegetables from pan and set aside.

4 Heat remaining vegetable oil in pan, add sauce mixture and bring to simmering, stirring constantly. Return fish and vegetables to pan, add spring onions and stir-fry for 1-2 minutes longer.

CHILLI CRABS

Crabs quickly cooked in hot oil then cooked with a Chilli and Onion Paste and finally moistened with a Peanut and Tomato Sauce.

Serves 4
2 uncooked crabs, cleaned and cut into quarters
vegetable oil for deep-frying
1 tomato, cut into wedges
1 egg, lightly beaten
½ lettuce, leaves separated

Chilli And Onion Paste
2 onions, roughly chopped
5 cm (2 inch) piece fresh ginger, peeled and roughly chopped
4 fresh red chillies, roughly chopped
5 cloves garlic, halved
2 tablespoons water

Peanut And Tomato Sauce
90 ml (3 fl oz) tomato sauce
2 tablespoons peanut butter
1 tablespoon cornflour
180 ml (6 fl oz) water
1 teaspoon dried shrimp powder
1 teaspoon salt
1 tablespoon muscovado or Demerara sugar
2 teaspoons light soy sauce

1 Lightly smash crab claws with cleaver and set aside.

2 To make paste, place onions, ginger, chillies, garlic and water in a food processor or blender and process to make a smooth paste. Set aside.

3 To make sauce, place tomato sauce, peanut butter,

cornflour, water, shrimp powder, salt, sugar and soy sauce in a bowl and mix to combine. Set aside.

4 Heat vegetable oil in a wok or large saucepan until a cube of bread, when dropped in, browns in 50 seconds. Cook crabs in batches for 3-4 minutes or until they just change colour. Remove crabs and drain on absorbent kitchen paper. Drain all but 2 tablespoons of oil from pan.

5 Heat reserved oil in wok or saucepan, add onion paste and stir-fry for 2-3 minutes. Add crabs and peanut sauce, bring to simmering and simmer for 4-5 minutes or until sauce just begins to thicken. Stir in tomato. Remove pan from heat and stir in egg. Line a large serving platter with lettuce leaves, top with crab mixture and serve immediately.

STIR-FRIED FISH
AND BROCCOLI

REALLY EASY!

**Stir-fried fish with crispy broccoli moistened with
a soy-flavoured sauce.**

Serves 4

300g (10 oz) boneless fish fillets, cut into large pieces
1¼ teaspoons salt
freshly ground black pepper
2 tablespoons plus ½ teaspoon cornflour
3 tablespoons vegetable oil
1 head broccoli, cut into small florets
2 cloves garlic, thinly sliced
1 small onion, cut into wedges
1 small skinned tomato, cut into wedges
125 ml (4 fl oz) water
1 tablespoon light soy sauce
¼ teaspoon sesame oil

1 Season fish fillets with ½ teaspoon salt and black
pepper to taste. Toss fish in 2 tablespoons cornflour.

2 Heat vegetable oil in a wok or frying pan over a
medium heat, add fish and cook, turning frequently, until
golden on both sides and flesh flakes when tested with a
fork. Remove fish from pan, set aside and keep warm.

3 Add broccoli, garlic and ¼ teaspoon salt to pan and
stir-fry for 3-4 minutes or until broccoli just changes colour.
Add onion and tomato to pan and stir-fry for 2-3 minutes
longer. Spoon vegetable mixture over fish and set aside.

4 Combine water, soy sauce, ½ teaspoon salt, ½ teaspoon
cornflour and sesame oil in a small bowl and mix together.
Stir cornflour mixture into pan and cook, stirring, for 1-2
minutes or until sauce boils and thickens slightly. Spoon
sauce over fish and vegetables and serve.

CHICKEN AND DUCK

Chicken and duck are very popular in China
and so there are many recipes which use them.
The most famous is, of course, Peking Duck. The
origins of this recipe go back to the Ming dynasty
when the method of cooking was very lengthy.
Here you will find an equally delicious,
but quickly made recipe, for this
well-loved dish.

EASY PEKING DUCK

This is a simplified method of preparing and cooking Peking Duck and although it may still seem time consuming, it is well worth the effort.

Serves 4
2.5kg (5 lb) duck
1.5 litres (2½ pints) water
2 teaspoons chopped fresh ginger
3 tablespoons brown sugar
3 spring onions, roughly chopped
1 cucumber, peeled, seeded and cut into 5 cm (2 inch) strips

Barbecue Sauce
2 tablespoons hoisin sauce
1 tablespoon water
½ teaspoon sesame oil
1 teaspoon brown sugar

Pancakes
125g (4 oz) plain flour
250 ml (8 fl oz) boiling water
1 tablespoon sesame oil

1 Rinse duck inside and out, then pat dry with kitchen paper. Place duck in front of a fan, or in a cool breezy place and leave to dry for 1 hour.

2 Place water in a large saucepan and bring to the boil. Add ginger, sugar and spring onions, then carefully lower duck into the water, making sure that the whole duck is covered. Remove duck immediately and discard liquid. Place duck in front of fan (or cool breezy place) again and leave to dry for an hour.

3 To make sauce, place hoisin sauce, water, sesame oil and sugar in a small pan, bring to the boil and cook, stirring, for 30 seconds. Remove pan from heat and set aside to cool.

4 Preheat oven to 180C,350F,Gas 4. Place duck on a roasting rack set in a baking dish and roast for 30 minutes in the preheated oven. Reduce oven temperature to 150C,300F,Gas 2, and cook for 1 hour longer. Then increase the oven temperature to 200C,400F,Gas 6 and cook until the skin of the duck is brown and crispy.

5 To make pancakes, sieve flour into a large bowl, then stir in boiling water and sesame oil and mix well. Knead dough until smooth then cover and leave to stand for 30 minutes. Shape dough into a roll and cut into about 16 pieces. Roll out each piece into a 10 cm (4 inch) circle and fry without fat in a non-stick frying pan until little bubbles appear on the surface, then turn over and cook the other side. Set aside and keep warm in a steamer until ready to serve.

6 To serve, remove all crispy skin from duck and cut into 4x6 cm (1½ x 2½ inch) pieces. Cut breast meat of duck into similar size pieces and arrange skin, meat, pancakes and cucumber on a serving platter. Put sauce into a serving bowl and serve with duck. To eat, spread a pancake with a teaspoon of sauce, top with a piece of skin, a piece of meat and a piece of cucumber. Roll up pancake and eat with your fingers.

SPICED DUCK

**A whole duck blanched and then allowed to cool
in a spicy stock, then left to marinate for 2 hours,
and finally deep-fried until crisp and golden.**

Serves 4

1 litre (1¾ pint) chicken stock
125 ml (4 fl oz) soy sauce
2 teaspoons finely chopped fresh ginger
2 cloves garlic, finely chopped
2 teaspoons five spice powder
1 x 2 kg (4 lb) duck
vegetable oil for deep-frying

Chilli Marinade

2 tablespoons sugar
2 tablespoons dry sherry
½ teaspoon five spice powder
½ teaspoon sesame oil
1 tablespoon soy sauce
1 teaspoon chilli sauce

1 Place stock, soy sauce, ginger, garlic and five spice powder in a large saucepan, cover and bring to the boil. Add duck, bring back to the boil and boil for 1 minute. Remove pan from heat and set aside to stand, covered, until liquid cools to room temperature.

2 To make marinade, place sugar, sherry, five spice powder, sesame oil, soy sauce and chilli sauce in a bowl and mix well to combine.

3 Remove duck from liquid and drain well. Cut duck in half through the breast and back bones and pat dry. Place duck, cut side down on a baking tray. Rub skin with marinade and set aside to marinate for 2 hours.

4 Heat oil in a large saucepan and cook half a duck at a time for 10 minutes or until golden brown and cooked through. Drain on absorbent kitchen paper. To serve, shred the duck flesh into small pieces with two forks.

LEMON CHICKEN

E A S Y !

**Bite-sized pieces of chicken cooked with
mushroom, green pepper, ginger, lemon rind,
spring onions and then moistened with a soy,
sherry and lemon juice sauce.**

Serves 6

6 dried Chinese mushrooms
1 teaspoon salt
freshly ground black pepper
5 tablespoons peanut (groundnut) oil
2 kg (4 lb) chicken thigh fillets, cut into bite-sized pieces
1 green pepper, chopped
1 teaspoon finely chopped fresh ginger
2 tablespoons finely grated lemon rind
4 spring onions, sliced
3 tablespoons dry sherry
2 tablespoons soy sauce
1 teaspoon cornflour
1 tablespoon water
1 tablespoon lemon juice

1 Place mushrooms in a bowl, cover with boiling water
and set aside to soak for 20 minutes or until mushrooms
are tender. Drain, remove stalks if necessary and chop
mushrooms.

2 Mix salt, black pepper to taste and 1 tablespoon oil to
a paste. Place chicken in a bowl, add salt and pepper
paste and mix well to coat chicken. Heat 3 tablespoons
oil in a wok or frying pan, add chicken and cook for 10
minutes or until chicken is just cooked. Remove chicken
from pan, set aside and keep warm.

3 Heat remaining oil in pan, add mushrooms, green
pepper, ginger, lemon rind and spring onions. Stir in

sherry and soy sauce and bring to the boil. Combine cornflour and water and stir into sauce. Return chicken to pan and cook for 5 minutes longer or until chicken is heated through. Stir in lemon juice and serve immediately.

LEMON CHICKEN

SMOKED CHICKEN

REALLY EASY!

A whole chicken cooked in a foil parcel in the aroma of Jasmine tea leaves. Chicken cooked in this way is moist with a crisp skin and a distinctive flavour.

Serves 6

125g (4 oz) sugar
3 tablespoons Jasmine tea leaves
2 tablespoons salt
1 x 1.5 kg (3 lb) chicken
freshly ground black pepper
1 tablespoon soy sauce
2 teaspoons sesame oil

1 Preheat oven to 190C,375F,Gas 5. Line a baking dish with sheets of aluminium foil large enough to completely enclose the chicken. Combine sugar, tea leaves and salt and spread out over foil. Place a roasting rack in the baking dish and place chicken on rack. Sprinkle chicken liberally with black pepper, bring foil up around chicken to completely enclose and bake in the oven for 1 hour.

2 Combine soy sauce and sesame oil. Open foil parcel, brush chicken with soy sauce mixture and bake, uncovered, for 20 minutes longer or until chicken is cooked through. To serve, cut into small pieces and serve immediately.

DUCK WITH BLACK BEAN SAUCE

EASY!

**Duck marinated in plum sauce and then cooked
in the oven and served with a Black Bean Sauce.
This dish looks great served on a bed of sliced
cucumber and garnished with shredded ginger
and fresh coriander.**

Serves 4
2 kg (4 lb) duck
90 ml (3 fl oz) Chinese plum sauce
½ teaspoon salt
1 cucumber, sliced

Black Bean Sauce
1 teaspoon sugar
1 tablespoon black bean garlic sauce
1 teaspoon sesame oil
4 tablespoons Chinese plum sauce
1 fresh red chilli, cut into thin strips

1 Cut duck down back and lay out flat. Wash and pat dry with absorbent kitchen paper. Place plum sauce and salt in a small bowl and mix to combine. Rub plum sauce mixture over duck and set aside to marinate for 30 minutes.

2 Preheat oven to 180C,350F,Gas 4. Place duck in a baking dish and bake for 1 hour or until cooked.

3 To make sauce, place sugar, bean sauce, sesame oil, plum sauce and chilli in a small bowl and mix to combine.

4 To serve, cut duck into pieces and accompany with sliced cucumber and Black Bean Sauce.

PO CHERO

E A S Y !

**An unusual dish of chicken, pork and Chinese
sausages cooked with sweet potato, chickpeas,
Chinese cabbage and tomato-flavoured chicken
stock.**

Serves 4

8 large Chinese dried mushrooms
2 tablespoons peanut (groundnut) oil
4 chicken drumsticks
350g (12 oz) pork fillets, cubed
4 Chinese sausages, cut into pieces
2 onions, sliced
2 cloves garlic, crushed
250g (8 oz) sweet potato, diced
300g (10 oz) canned chickpeas, drained
500 ml (16 fl oz) chicken stock
2 tablespoons tomato purée
1 tablespoon soy sauce
1 tablespoon cornflour
2 tablespoons water
¼ Chinese cabbage, roughly chopped

1 Place mushrooms in a bowl, cover with boiling water
and set aside to soak for 20 minutes or until mushrooms
are tender. Drain, remove stalks if necessary and cut
mushrooms in half.

2 Heat oil in a large frying pan, add chicken and cook,
turning frequently until brown on all sides. Remove
chicken from pan and set aside. Cook pork and sausages
in the same way.

3 Return chicken, pork and sausages to pan, add
mushrooms, onions, garlic, sweet potato and chickpeas
and mix to combine. Combine stock, tomato purée and

soy sauce, add to pan, cover and cook over a low heat for 30 minutes or until meat and vegetables are cooked through and tender.

4 Combine cornflour and water. Stir cabbage and cornflour mixture into meat and vegetable mixture and cook, stirring constantly, until sauce boils and thickens. Serve immediately.

CRISPY CHICKEN WINGS

REALLY EASY!

**Chicken wings marinated in salt, sugar and soy
sauce, then deep fried until crisp.**

Serves 4

1½ teaspoons salt
1 teaspoon light soy sauce
½ teaspoon sugar
½ teaspoon Chinese rice wine
16 large chicken wings, cut at joints
vegetable oil for deep-frying

1 Place salt, soy sauce, sugar and wine in a bowl and mix to combine. Add chicken, toss to coat and set aside to marinate for 10-15 minutes.

2 Heat oil in a wok or large saucepan until a cube of bread, when dropped in, browns in 50 seconds. Cook chicken wings for 5 minutes or until golden, crisp and cooked through.

BRAISED CHICKEN WITH CHESTNUTS

EASY!

A rich stir-fry of chicken and chestnuts. If the mixture seems too dry add a little more water during cooking.

Serves 4

75g (2½ oz) dried chestnuts
2 tablespoons vegetable oil
500g (1 lb) boneless chicken breast fillets, cut into bite-sized pieces
1 cm (½ inch) piece fresh ginger, grated
1 tablespoon dark soy sauce
1 tablespoon light soy sauce
2 teaspoons salt
1¾ teaspoons sugar
½ teaspoon sesame oil
300 ml (10 fl oz) water

1 Place chestnuts in a bowl and pour over enough hot water to cover. Set aside to soak for 30 minutes or until chestnuts are soft. Using the tip of a small sharp knife carefully remove skin from chestnuts, drain well and set aside.

2 Heat vegetable oil in a wok or frying pan over a high heat, add chicken and ginger and stir-fry for 3-4 minutes or until chicken changes colour. Stir chestnuts, dark soy sauce , light soy sauce, salt, sugar, sesame oil and water into pan, cover and bring to a gentle boil. Reduce heat to low and simmer, stirring occasionally, for 15 minutes or until chicken and chestnuts are tender.

CRISPY CHICKEN WINGS • BRAISED CHICKEN WITH CHESTNUTS

FRAGRANT STEAMED CHICKEN

E A S Y !

**Cloud ears, also known as wood ears, are
black fungi available from Oriental food stores.
Like dried Chinese mushrooms, they have to be
soaked in hot water until they are tender before
using. If they are unavailable, use two
extra dried mushrooms.**

Serves 4

3 dried Chinese mushrooms, stalks removed
1 tablespoon cloud ear fungi
60 ml (2 fl oz) oyster sauce
60 ml (2 fl oz) vegetable oil
1 tablespoon water
1 teaspoon light soy sauce
1 teaspoon sugar
½ teaspoon salt
¼ teaspoon freshly ground black pepper
1 teaspoon sesame oil
4 boneless chicken breast fillets, sliced
8 thin slices peeled fresh ginger
2 fresh red chillies, seeded and cut into thin strips
2 tablespoons shredded spring onions

1 Place dried mushrooms and fungi in separate bowls,
pour over enough boiling water to cover and set aside to
stand for 20 minutes or until tender. Drain, rinse under
cold running water and cut into thin strips.

2 Place oyster sauce, vegetable oil, water, soy sauce,
sugar, salt, black pepper and sesame oil in a bowl and
mix to combine. Add chicken, mushrooms and fungi and
mix to combine. Place chicken mixture on one or two
lightly-oiled heatproof plates, sprinkle with ginger and

chillies and set aside to marinate for 10 minutes.

3 Place plates of prepared chicken mixture in a bamboo steamer set over a saucepan of simmering water, cover and steam for 10 minutes or until chicken is cooked. Sprinkle with spring onions and serve immediately.

FRAGRANT STEAMED CHICKEN

CHICKEN IN RED BEAN CURD

EASY!

Chicken wings coated in red bean curd and chilli and deep-fried until crisp.

Serves 6

5 cm (2 inch) piece red bean curd
½ teaspoon sugar
½ teaspoon salt
1 teaspoon chilli powder
1 kg (2 lb) chicken wings, cut at joints
2 tablespoons cornflour
vegetable oil for deep-frying

1 Place red bean curd, sugar, salt and chilli powder in a bowl and mash to combine. Add chicken, toss to coat and set aside to marinate for 30 minutes.

2 Place chicken and cornflour in a plastic food bag, shake to coat chicken with cornflour. Shake off excess cornflour.

3 Heat oil in wok or large saucepan until a cube of bread, when dropped in, browns in 50 seconds. Deep-fry chicken in batches for 5 minutes or until golden and crisp and cooked through. Remove from pan, drain on absorbent kitchen paper and serve immediately.

BRAISED GINGER CHICKEN

REALLY EASY!

A quick dish of chicken stir-fried with red and green peppers, onion, garlic and ginger.

Serves 4

2 tablespoons vegetable oil
500g (1 lb) boneless chicken breast fillets, cut into strips
1 red pepper, cut into rings
1 green pepper, cut into rings
1 onion, cut into eighths
2 cloves garlic, crushed
2 teaspoons grated fresh ginger
1 tablespoon cornflour
1 tablespoon sherry
2 teaspoons soy sauce
300 ml (10 fl oz) chicken stock

1 Heat oil in a wok or frying pan and stir-fry chicken in batches for 3-4 minutes or until brown. Remove chicken from pan and set aside.

2 Add red and green peppers, onion, garlic and ginger and stir-fry for 4-5 minutes or until peppers and onion are soft. Combine cornflour, sherry, soy sauce and stock. Return chicken to pan and stir in cornflour mixture. Cook, stirring constantly, for 2-3 minutes or until mixture boils and thickens and chicken is heated through. Serve immediately.

STIR-FRIED
SESAME CHICKEN

EASY!

The easiest way to toast a small quantity of sesame seeds is to place them in a small frying pan and heat over a medium heat. Shake the pan frequently, until seeds pop and are golden. Take care they do not burn.

Serves 4

90 ml (3 fl oz) water
1 teaspoon cornflour
1 teaspoon dark soy sauce
2 tablespoons sesame oil
½ teaspoon salt
½ teaspoon sugar
500g (1 lb) boneless chicken breast fillets, cut into
5 cm (2 inch) strips
2 tablespoons vegetable oil
5 cm (2 inch) piece peeled fresh ginger, cut into thin strips
1 teaspoon Chinese rice wine
1 tablespoon sesame seeds, toasted
3 spring onions, cut into 5 cm (2 inch) lengths

1 Place 1 tablespoon water, cornflour, soy sauce, 1 teaspoon sesame oil, salt and sugar in a bowl and mix to combine. Add chicken, toss to coat and set aside to marinate for 10-15 minutes.

2 Heat vegetable oil in a wok or frying pan over a medium heat, add ginger and stir-fry for 2-3 minutes or until fragrant and crispy. Add chicken mixture and stir-fry for 3-4 minutes or until chicken changes colour. Stir in remaining water, remaining sesame oil and wine and stir-fry for 3-4 minutes longer or until chicken is cooked through. Sprinkle with sesame seeds and spring onions and serve immediately.

CHICKEN
IN OYSTER SAUCE

REALLY EASY!

**Chicken stir-fried with chillies and ginger and
then cooked in an oyster sauce.**

Serves 4

2½ tablespoons vegetable oil
500g (1 lb) chicken pieces, chopped into bite-sized pieces
4 fresh green chillies, cut into 1 cm (½ inch) pieces
3 thin slices peeled fresh ginger
90 ml (3 fl oz) oyster sauce
1 teaspoon dark soy sauce
½ teaspoon sugar
½ teaspoon salt
2 cloves garlic, sliced
2 spring onions, sliced diagonally
2 tablespoons chopped fresh coriander

1 Heat oil in a wok or frying pan over a high heat. Add
chicken, chillies and ginger and stir-fry for 3-4 minutes or
until chicken is golden.

2 Stir in oyster sauce, soy sauce, sugar, salt and garlic
and stir-fry for 3-4 minutes longer or until chicken is
cooked. Sprinkle with spring onions and coriander and
serve immediately.

STIR-FRIED SESAME CHICKEN • CHICKEN IN OYSTER SAUCE

CHICKEN AND CAULIFLOWER STIR-FRY

EASY!

Marinated chicken slices stir-fried with cauliflower, celery, carrot and tomato.

Serves 4

1¼ teaspoons salt
½ teaspoon cornflour
1 teaspoon light soy sauce
¼ teaspoon sugar
½ teaspoon sesame oil
250g (8 oz) boneless chicken breast fillets, sliced
60 ml (2 fl oz) vegetable oil
3 cloves garlic, thinly sliced
½ cauliflower, broken into small florets
2 tablespoons water
2 stalks celery, sliced diagonally
1 carrot, sliced
1 tomato, sliced
60 ml (2 fl oz) water blended with ½ teaspoon cornflour

1 Combine ½ teaspoon salt, cornflour, ½ teaspoon soy sauce, sugar and ¼ teaspoon sesame oil in a bowl. Add chicken, toss and set aside to marinate for 10-15 minutes.

2 Heat 2 tablespoons vegetable oil in a wok or frying pan over a medium heat, add chicken and garlic and stir-fry for 4-5 minutes. Remove chicken mixture from pan and set aside.

3 Add remaining vegetable oil, cauliflower, ¼ teaspoon salt and water to pan and stir-fry for 3-4 minutes or until cauliflower is tender. Add celery, carrot and tomato and return chicken to pan and stir-fry for 3-4 minutes longer or until carrot is tender.

4 Combine remaining salt, remaining soy sauce and remaining sesame oil with cornflour mixture. Push chicken and vegetables to one side and stir soy sauce mixture into pan. When mixture boils, push chicken and vegetables into sauce and toss to combine.

35 SESAME AND SOY CHICKEN

EASY!

**Chicken thighs marinated in soy sauce and
sesame oil, then stir-fried with spices, served
with tomato, cucumber and pineapple.**

Serves 2

1 tablespoon dark soy sauce
1½ teaspoons sesame oil
4 chicken thighs
1 teaspoon sugar
½ teaspoon salt
1 tablespoon light soy sauce
125 ml (4 fl oz) water
2 tablespoons vegetable oil
1 star anise
2 whole cloves
3 thin slices peeled fresh ginger
2 cloves garlic, crushed
1 spring onion, cut into 2.5 cm (1 inch) pieces
1 tomato, sliced
¼ cucumber, sliced
4 slices canned pineapple, drained and cut in quarters

1 Combine dark soy sauce and ½ teaspoon sesame oil,
rub evenly over chicken thighs and set aside to marinate
for 10-15 minutes. Place sugar, salt, remaining sesame
oil, light soy sauce and water in a bowl, mix to combine
and set aside.

2 Heat vegetable oil in a wok or frying pan over a
medium heat, add star anise, cloves, ginger and garlic and
stir-fry for 1-2 minutes. Add chicken mixture to pan and
stir-fry for 5 minutes. Stir soy sauce mixture and spring
onion into pan and simmer for 10 minutes or until chicken
is cooked. Remove star anise, cloves, ginger and garlic.
Serve garnished with tomato, cucumber and pineapple.

STIR-FRIED CHICKEN WITH CASHEWS

REALLY EASY!

Chicken strips stir-fried with onion, carrot, broccoli and cashews.

Serves 4

2 tablespoons vegetable oil
1 red onion, cut into wedges, separated
1 carrot, sliced diagonally
1 clove garlic, crushed
1 teaspoon grated fresh ginger
350g (12 oz) boneless chicken breast fillets, cut into strips
1 head broccoli, cut into florets
60g (2 oz) unsalted cashews
125 ml (4 fl oz) chicken stock
2 teaspoons cornflour
2 teaspoons soy sauce
1 tablespoon dry sherry
¼ teaspoon sesame oil
3 spring onions, sliced diagonally

1 Heat 1 tablespoon vegetable oil in a wok or frying pan, add onion, carrot, garlic and ginger and stir-fry for 5 minutes. Remove vegetable mixture and set aside.

2 Cook chicken in batches in pan for 2-3 minutes or until lightly browned. Remove and set aside.

3 Heat remaining vegetable oil in pan, add broccoli and cashews and stir-fry until broccoli just changes colour and cashews are golden.

4 Combine stock, cornflour, soy sauce, sherry and sesame oil. Return vegetables and chicken to pan, add cornflour mixture and cook, stirring, for 3-4 minutes or until sauce boils and thickens. Stir in spring onions and serve.

SESAME AND SOY CHICKEN • STIR-FRIED CHICKEN WITH CASHEWS

PORK AND LAMB

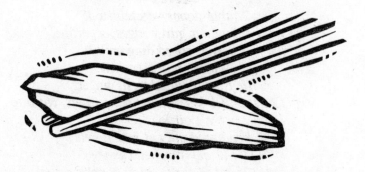

The most popular meat in China has to be pork, which features in many of the well-loved recipes such as Sweet and Sour, Spare ribs and Chop Suey. Pork is very versatile and adapts itself to many different types of cooking, rather like chicken, and in fact chicken and pork are interchangeable in most recipes. This chapter also includes a few recipes for lamb, which is less commonly used in Chinese cooking.

PORK RIBS
IN OYSTER SAUCE

EASY!

**Pork ribs marinated in garlic and oyster sauce
and then deep-fried until crisp and golden.**

Serves 4

*1½ tablespoons oyster sauce
2 cloves garlic, crushed
¼ teaspoon sugar
½ teaspoon chilli powder
1½ teaspoons light soy sauce
500g (1 lb) pork spare ribs, separated
vegetable oil for deep-frying
2 tablespoons water*

1 Place oyster sauce, garlic, sugar, chilli powder and light soy sauce in a bowl and mix well to combine. Add ribs and set aside to marinate for 1 hour. Drain and reserve marinade.

2 Heat oil in a wok or large saucepan until a cube of bread, when dropped in, browns in 50 seconds, and cook ribs in batches for 4-5 minutes or until golden and crispy. Remove ribs, drain on absorbent kitchen paper, set aside and keep warm.

3 Drain pan of all but 2 teaspoons oil, add reserved marinade and water and cook, stirring, for 3-4 minutes or until sauce begins to simmer. Serve as a dipping sauce with ribs.

STIR-FRIED BARBECUED PORK

EASY!

Barbecued pork cooked with ginger, mushrooms, peppers, mangetout and bamboo shoots and served on top of sweet and sour noodles.

Serves 4

10 dried Chinese mushrooms
350g (12 oz) rice noodles
1 tablespoon sesame oil
250g (8 oz) Chinese barbecued pork, (or cold roast pork), cut into thin strips
1 tablespoon grated fresh ginger
1 red, green or yellow pepper, cut into strips
125g (4 oz) mangetout
60g (2 oz) canned bamboo shoots, drained and sliced
2 tablespoons clear honey
60 ml (2 fl oz) soy sauce
1 tablespoon red wine vinegar

1 Place mushrooms in a bowl, cover with boiling water and soak for 20 minutes or until mushrooms are tender. Drain, remove stalks if necessary and slice mushrooms.

2 Cook noodles in boiling water following packet directions. Drain, set aside and keep warm.

3 Heat oil in a wok or frying pan, add pork, ginger and mushrooms and stir-fry for 2 minutes. Add red, green or yellow pepper, mangetout and bamboo shoots, and stir-fry for 1 minute longer. Remove pork and vegetable mixture from pan, set aside and keep warm.

4 Add honey, soy sauce and vinegar to pan and cook, stirring, until mixture boils. Add noodles and toss to coat with honey mixture. Serve noodles topped with pork and vegetable mixture.

CRISPY SAFFRON PORK

REALLY EASY!

Slices of belly pork tossed in a spicy marinade and then stir-fried until golden.

Serves 4

1 egg, beaten
3 tablespoons light soy sauce
¾ teaspoon sugar
½ teaspoon salt
½ teaspoon chilli powder
½ teaspoon vinegar
¼ teaspoon saffron powder
500g (1 lb) belly pork, skin removed, sliced
2 tablespoons vegetable oil
¼ lettuce, shredded

1 Place egg, 1 tablespoon soy sauce, sugar, salt, chilli powder, vinegar and saffron in a bowl and whisk to combine. Add pork, toss to combine and set aside to marinate for 10-15 minutes.

2 Heat oil in a wok over a high heat, add pork mixture and stir-fry for 7-10 minutes or until golden and cooked through. Switch off heat and stir in remaining soy sauce. Line a serving platter with lettuce, top with pork mixture and serve immediately.

STIR-FRIED BARBECUED PORK • CRISPY SAFFRON PORK

HONEY PORK

EASY!

**Whole pork fillets marinated with tomato
sauce, honey, five spice powder and soy
sauce and then baked in the oven. Served
in thick slices with cooked broccoli
and a Sherry Sauce.**

Serves 4

*500g (1 lb) pork fillets
1 tablespoon tomato sauce
2 tablespoons honey
¼ teaspoon five spice powder
2 teaspoons soy sauce
large head broccoli, broken into florets*

Sherry Sauce

*2 teaspoons cornflour
125 ml (4 fl oz) chicken stock
1 tablespoon dry sherry
1 teaspoon sugar
½ teaspoon oyster sauce*

1 Place pork fillets in a shallow glass or ceramic dish.
Place tomato sauce, 1 tablespoon honey, five spice
powder and soy sauce in a small bowl, mix to combine,
pour over pork, cover and set aside to marinate for
1 hour.

2 Preheat oven to 180C,350F,Gas 4. Drain pork, place
in a baking dish and bake for 20 minutes. Brush fillets
with remaining honey and bake for 10 minutes longer.

3 Boil, steam or microwave broccoli until just tender.

4 To make sauce, place cornflour, stock, sherry, sugar
and oyster sauce in a small saucepan and cook over a
medium heat, stirring, until sauce boils and thickens.

5 To serve, cut pork in thick slices and arrange on a serving platter. Surround with broccoli and spoon over sauce.

PORK WITH CUCUMBER

R E A L L Y   E A S Y !

Lean diced pork stir-fried with cucumber, spring onions, ginger and chillies and moistened with Sesame Sauce.

Serves 4
300g (10 oz) lean diced pork
2 tablespoons soy sauce
1 teaspoon cornflour
2 tablespoons peanut (groundnut) oil
2 small cucumbers, diced
2 spring onions, sliced
1 teaspoon finely sliced peeled fresh ginger
2 fresh red chillies, seeded and chopped

Sesame Sauce
1 teaspoon sugar
2 teaspoons red wine vinegar
1 tablespoon soy sauce
½ teaspoon cornflour
2 tablespoons water
1 tablespoon sesame oil

1 Place pork, soy sauce and cornflour in a bowl and mix to combine.

2 Heat oil in a wok or frying pan, add meat mixture and cucumbers and stir-fry for 3-4 minutes or until meat browns. Remove meat mixture from pan and set aside.

3 Add spring onions, ginger and chillies to pan and stir-fry for 1-2 minutes. Return pork mixture to pan and stir-fry for 5 minutes longer or until pork is cooked through.

4 To make sauce, combine sugar, vinegar, soy sauce,

cornflour, water and sesame oil and stir into pan. Cook, stirring constantly, for 2-3 minutes or until sauce boils and thickens. Serve immediately.

PORK WITH MUSHROOMS

REALLY EASY!

Minced pork cooked with water chestnuts, peas, celery, and sherry and soy sauce to moisten, topped with chopped toasted almonds.

Serves 2

4 dried Chinese mushrooms
1 tablespoon vegetable oil
30g (1 oz) blanched almonds
250g (8 oz) lean pork mince
2 tablespoons soy sauce
2 teaspoons cornflour
1 teaspoon sugar
2 tablespoons water
freshly ground black pepper
1 tablespoon dry sherry
8 canned water chestnuts, drained and finely chopped
60g (2 oz) fresh or frozen peas
2 stalks celery, diced
1 clove garlic, chopped
2 slices fresh ginger

1 Place mushrooms in a bowl, cover with boiling water and set aside to soak for 20 minutes or until mushrooms are tender. Drain and reserve liquid. Remove stalks from mushrooms if necessary and chop mushrooms finely.

2 Heat half the oil in a wok or frying pan, add almonds and stir-fry for 1-2 minutes or until golden. Remove and drain on absorbent kitchen paper, then chop finely.

3 Place pork, half the soy sauce, 1 teaspoon cornflour, sugar, water and black pepper to taste, in a bowl and mix well to combine. In a separate bowl combine sherry, remaining soy sauce and cornflour, and reserved mushroom liquid.

4 Add remaining oil to pan and heat. Add water chestnuts, peas and celery, cover and cook for 2-3 minutes. Remove vegetable mixture and set aside. Add garlic, ginger and pork mixture to pan and stir-fry for 2 minutes. Reduce heat, cover and simmer for 5 minutes. Add vegetable mixture, pour in sherry mixture and cook, stirring constantly, until mixture boils and thickens. Sprinkle with almonds and serve immediately.

PORK WITH MUSHROOMS

SWEET AND SOUR PORK

**Another well loved classic – pieces of pork
coated in batter and then deep-fried and served
with Sweet and Sour Sauce.**

Serves 4
2 egg yolks
1 tablespoon water
2 tablespoons cornflour
500g (1 lb) pork fillet cut into 2 cm (¾ inch) cubes
vegetable oil for deep-frying

Sweet And Sour Sauce
1 tablespoon vegetable oil
1 onion, cut into eighths
½ red pepper, cut into 2.5 cm (1 inch) pieces
½ green pepper, cut into 2.5 cm (1 inch) pieces
1 tablespoon cornflour
125 ml (4 fl oz) water
2 tablespoons tomato sauce
2 teaspoons soy sauce
1 tablespoon white vinegar
*350g (11oz) can pineapple pieces, drained and juice
reserved*

1 Combine egg yolks and water. Place cornflour in a
bowl and gradually stir in egg yolk mixture. Add pork
and toss to coat.

2 Heat oil in a wok or large saucepan until a cube of
bread, when dropped in, browns in 50 seconds, and
cook pork in batches for 7-10 minutes or until golden
and cooked through. Remove pork and drain on kitchen
paper.

3 To make sauce, heat oil in a wok or frying pan, add
onion and red and green pepper and stir-fry for

5 minutes or until vegetables are soft. Combine corn-flour, water, tomato sauce, soy sauce, vinegar, and reserved pineapple juice and stir into pan. Cook, stirring constantly, for 2-3 minutes or until sauce boils and thickens.

4 Stir pork and pineapple pieces into sauce and cook for 3-4 minutes longer or until heated through. Serve immediately.

CHINESE SPARE RIBS

EASY!

One of the most popular of chinese dishes, these ribs can also be served as a starter.

Serves 4

8 pork spare ribs, trimmed of rind and excess fat
60 ml (2 fl oz) dry sherry
2 tablespoons honey
2 tablespoons plum sauce
60 ml (2 fl oz) tomato sauce
2 fresh red chillies, seeded and chopped
2 cloves garlic, crushed
1 tablespoon grated fresh ginger
½ teaspoon five spice powder

1 Cut each spare rib into 3 pieces and place in a bowl. Combine sherry, honey, plum sauce, tomato sauce, chillies, garlic, ginger and five spice powder and pour over ribs. Mix well to coat ribs.

2 Place ribs and sauce mixture in a large frying pan, cover and cook over a low heat, stirring occasionally, for 1 hour or until pork is tender and glazed.

CHOP SUEY

REALLY EASY!

A mixture of pork and chicken stir-fried with chopped cabbage, beans, celery, onions, carrot, bamboo shoots and prawns. Traditionally served with rice or noodles.

Serves 6

2 tablespoons vegetable oil
250g (8 oz) lean pork mince
½ Chinese cabbage, shredded
125g (4 oz) green beans, sliced diagonally
2 sticks celery, sliced diagonally
2 onions, chopped
1 carrot, chopped
250 ml (8 fl oz) chicken stock
2 teaspoons cornflour
1 tablespoon soy sauce
2 boneless chicken breast fillets, cooked and cut into cubes
250g (8 oz) uncooked prawns, peeled and deveined
250g (8 oz) can bamboo shoots

1 Heat oil in a wok or large frying pan, add pork and stir-fry for 5 minutes or until browned.

2 Add cabbage, beans, celery, onions and carrot and stir-fry for 3-4 minutes. Place stock, cornflour and soy sauce in a small bowl and whisk to combine. Stir cornflour mixture into meat mixture and cook, stirring, for 3-4 minutes or until mixture boils and thickens.

3 Add chicken, prawns and bamboo shoots to pan and cook for 3-4 minutes longer or until prawns are cooked. Serve immediately.

CHINESE SPARE RIBS • CHOP SUEY

SPICED PORK FILLET

REALLY EASY!

**Whole pork fillets marinated in a mixture of
hoisin sauce, soy sauce, vinegar, sherry, ginger
and honey, baked in the oven and served sliced
with a sauce made from the marinade.**

Serves 4
500g (1 lb) pork fillets
125 ml (4 fl oz) chicken stock
2 teaspoons cornflour

Ginger Marinade
2 tablespoons hoisin sauce
1 tablespoon soy sauce
2 teaspoons vinegar
2 tablespoons dry sherry
1 teaspoon grated fresh ginger
2 tablespoons clear honey

1 Place pork fillets in a shallow glass or ceramic dish. To make marinade, place hoisin sauce, soy sauce, vinegar, sherry, ginger and honey in a small bowl, mix to combine. Pour marinade over pork, cover and set aside for 1 hour.

2 Preheat oven to 180C, 350F, Gas 4. Drain pork and reserve marinade. Place pork in a baking dish and cook for 30 minutes in the preheated oven, turning several times.

3 Place reserved marinade, stock and cornflour in a saucepan and cook, stirring until sauce boils and thickens. To serve, slice pork and spoon sauce over slices.

PORK WITH NOODLES

REALLY EASY!

Sliced pork fillet and vegetables stir-fried and then tossed with rice noodles and chilli sauce.

Serves 4
300g (10 oz) pork fillet, sliced
1 tablespoon soy sauce
150g (5 oz) rice noodles
2 tablespoons peanut (groundnut) oil
½ onion, sliced
1 green pepper, chopped
½ cauliflower, broken into florets
2 tablespoons water
½ teaspoon chilli sauce

1 Place pork and soy sauce in a bowl and toss to combine.

2 Soak noodles in hot water for 15 minutes or until soft. Drain and set aside.

3 Heat 1 tablespoon oil in a wok or frying pan, add pork and stir-fry for 2 minutes. Remove pork from pan and set aside. Add remaining oil, onion, green pepper and cauliflower and stir-fry for 2 minutes. Add water, cover pan and simmer for 5 minutes or until cauliflower is just tender.

4 Return pork to pan, add noodles and chilli sauce and stir-fry for 2-3 minutes or until heated through. Serve immediately.

SPICED PORK FILLET • PORK WITH NOODLES

109

PORK STIR-FRY

REALLY EASY!

**A quick stir-fry of pork, green beans, red pepper
and toasted sesame seeds.**

Serves 4

1 tablespoon vegetable oil
250g (8 oz) lean diced pork
1 clove garlic, crushed
2 tablespoons soy sauce
freshly ground black pepper
500g (1 lb) green beans, cut into 2 cm (¾ inch) lengths
1 red pepper, cut into strips
6 spring onions, cut into 5 cm (2 inch) lengths
½ teaspoon sesame oil
2 tablespoons toasted sesame seeds

1 Heat oil in a wok or frying pan, add pork and garlic
and stir-fry for 3-4 minutes or until pork changes colour.
Add soy sauce, black pepper to taste, beans and red
pepper, and stir-fry for 2-3 minutes.

2 Reduce heat, cover pan and simmer for 20 minutes or
until pork is tender. Stir in spring onions, sesame oil and
sesame seeds and serve immediately.

HOT SPICY PORK

REALLY EASY!

A hot spicy stir-fry of pork, five spice powder, chilli and oyster sauce and lemon juice.

Serves 6

1kg (2 lb) pork fillet, cut into thin strips
2 tablespoons cornflour
½ teaspoon five spice powder
2 tablespoons vegetable oil
1 teaspoon grated fresh ginger
2 tablespoons clear honey
2 teaspoons cornflour blended with 4 tablespoons water
2 teaspoons hot chilli sauce
2 teaspoons oyster sauce
4 tablespoons lemon juice

1 Toss meat strips in combined cornflour and five spice powder. Heat oil in a wok or large frying pan and stir-fry pork mixture over high heat for 3-4 minutes until pork is well browned.

2 Add grated ginger and honey to pan and cook gently for 1 minute. Pour in blended cornflour, chilli sauce, oyster sauce and lemon juice. Stir until sauce boils and thickens. Serve at once.

STIR-FRIED LAMB

R E A L L Y   E A S Y !

Thinly sliced lamb quickly cooked with onions, garlic, sherry and soy sauce.

Serves 4
500g (1 lb) lamb fillets, thinly sliced
1 tablespoon cornflour
2 tablespoons vegetable oil
3 onions, sliced
2 cloves garlic, crushed
2 tablespoons dry sherry
1 tablespoon soy sauce

1 Toss lamb in cornflour to coat. Heat 1 tablespoon oil in a wok or frying pan, add lamb and stir-fry for 4-5 minutes or until browned. Remove lamb from pan and set aside.

2 Heat remaining oil in pan, add onions and garlic and stir-fry for 5 minutes or until onions are soft. Stir in sherry and soy sauce, return lamb to pan and cook, stirring, for 2-3 minutes longer or until heated through.

LAMB WITH BAMBOO SHOOTS

EASY!

**Lamb steaks cooked in spicy stock until tender,
then shredded and stir-fried with spring onions
and bamboo shoots and served on noodles.**

Serves 4

2 tablespoons vegetable oil
4 lean lamb leg steaks, trimmed of all visible fat
8 spring onions, chopped
2 cloves garlic, crushed
250 ml (8 fl oz) beef stock
1 tablespoon soy sauce
1 teaspoon chilli paste (sambal oelek)
60 ml (2 fl oz) white wine
1 teaspoon five spice powder
125g (4 oz) canned bamboo shoots, drained and sliced
250g (8 oz) rice noodles

1 Heat 1 tablespoon oil in a large frying pan, add steaks and cook for 2-3 minutes on each side or until browned. Transfer steaks to a large saucepan. Add three-quarters of the spring onions and garlic to frying pan and stir-fry for 2 minutes, then add to saucepan with lamb.

2 Add stock, soy sauce, chilli paste (sambal oelek), wine and five spice powder to lamb, bring to the boil, reduce heat, cover and simmer for 1 hour or until lamb is tender. Remove lamb from cooking liquid, set aside to cool, then shred meat. Drain cooking liquid and discard solids.

3 Heat remaining oil in frying pan, add remaining spring onions and stir-fry for 2 minutes. Add shredded lamb and bamboo shoots and stir-fry for 1 minute longer. Add a little cooking liquid to moisten.

4 Cook noodles in boiling water following packet directions, drain, spoon meat mixture over noodles and serve immediately.

STIR-FRIED LAMB • LAMB WITH BAMBOO SHOOTS

113

ORIENTAL LAMB

REALLY EASY!

Thin strips of lamb cooked with spinach and ginger.

Serves 4

500g (1 lb)lean lamb leg steaks, cut into thin strips
2 tablespoons oyster sauce
2 tablespoons dry white wine
1 teaspoon sugar
½ teaspoon sesame oil
2 tablespoons vegetable oil
500g (1 lb) spinach, leaves removed and cut into large pieces, stalks cut into 2.5 cm (1 inch) pieces
2 teaspoons grated fresh ginger
½ teaspoon cornflour blended with 60 ml (2 fl oz) chicken stock

1 Place lamb, oyster sauce, wine, sugar and sesame oil in a bowl and toss to combine. Cover and set aside to marinate for 20 minutes.

2 Heat oil in a wok or frying pan, add lamb mixture and stir-fry in batches for 2-3 minutes or until meat browns. Remove meat from pan and set aside.

3 Add spinach stalks and ginger to pan and stir-fry for 3 minutes or until stalks are just tender. Return meat to pan, add spinach leaves and cornflour mixture and cook, stirring constantly, for 3-4 minutes or until spinach leaves start to wilt. Serve immediately.

BEEF DISHES

**Chinese dishes are quickly cooked and rely on
first-rate ingredients, so when cooking beef
recipes always buy the best quality meat.
This selection of recipes includes stir-fries,
braised and roasted dishes.**

CLAY POT BEEF

E A S Y !

**Small slivers of beef cooked with a Sherry Sauce,
in a clay pot or casserole on top of the stove.**

Serves 4

1 teaspoon freshly ground black pepper
½ teaspoon cornflour
¼ teaspoon sugar
¼ teaspoon salt
2 tablespoons water
500g (1 lb) topside beef, cut into thin strips
2 tablespoons vegetable oil
3 thin slices peeled fresh ginger
2 cloves garlic, thinly sliced
½ carrot, sliced diagonally
60g (2 oz) straw mushrooms, halved
60g (2 oz) canned bamboo shoots, sliced
60g (2 oz) mangetout

Sherry Sauce

2 tablespoons water
1 tablespoon oyster sauce
1 tablespoon semi-sweet sherry
1 tablespoon light soy sauce
½ teaspoon cornflour
½ teaspoon sugar
¼ teaspoon salt

1 Place black pepper, cornflour, sugar, salt and water in a bowl and mix to combine. Add beef, toss to combine and set aside to marinate for 10-15 minutes.

2 To make sauce, place water, oyster sauce, sherry, soy sauce, cornflour, sugar and salt in a bowl and mix to combine. Set aside.

3 Place oil and ginger in a clay pot or flameproof casserole dish and heat over a medium heat for 2-3 minutes or until hot. Add garlic and beef mixture and stir-fry over a high heat for 4-5 minutes or until almost cooked. Add carrot, mushrooms, bamboo shoots, mangetout and Sherry Sauce, mix to combine and cover. Turn off heat and leave for 1-2 minutes, before serving.

CLAY POT BEEF

STIR-FRIED BEEF AND BABY CORN

REALLY EASY!

Strips of beef stir-fried with mushrooms, carrots, baby sweetcorn and green beans and served in a Sesame and Soy Sauce.

Serves 4

¼ teaspoon salt
¼ teaspoon sugar
¼ teaspoon freshly ground black pepper
2 teaspoons water
1½ teaspoons light soy sauce
½ teaspoon sesame oil
1 teaspoon cornflour
½ teaspoon bicarbonate of soda
3 tablespoons vegetable oil
125g (4 oz) topside beef, cut into thin strips
200g (7 oz) canned straw mushrooms, sliced
2 carrots, cut into 5 cm (2 inch) strips
300g (10 oz) canned baby sweet corn, drained and sliced
1 large onion, sliced
125g (4 oz) green beans, cut into 5 cm (2 inch) pieces
3 spring onions, cut into 5 cm (2 inch) lengths
4 cloves garlic, thinly sliced
1 tablespoon dry sherry

Sesame And Soy Sauce

½ teaspoon cornflour
½ teaspoon salt
¼ teaspoon sugar
90 ml (3 fl oz) water
½ teaspoon light soy sauce
¼ teaspoon sesame oil

1 Place salt, sugar, black pepper, water, soy sauce, sesame oil, cornflour, bicarbonate of soda and 1 teaspoon vegetable oil in a bowl and mix to combine. Add beef, toss to combine and set aside to marinate for 10-15 minutes.

2 To make sauce, place cornflour, salt, sugar, water, soy sauce and sesame oil in a small bowl and mix to combine. Set aside.

3 Heat remaining vegetable oil in a wok or frying pan over a high heat, add beef mixture and stir-fry for 2-3 minutes or until beef just changes colour. Remove beef from pan and set aside. Add mushrooms, carrots, sweet corn, onion, beans, spring onions and garlic and stir-fry for 3-4 minutes or until vegetables are almost cooked. Return beef to pan, add sauce and stir-fry for 2-3 minutes longer or until heated through. Stir in sherry and serve immediately.

STIR-FRIED BEEF AND BABY CORN

BEEF IN OYSTER SAUCE

E A S Y !

Strips of beef marinated in soy sauce and rice wine. Then deep fried before being stir-fried with mangetout, carrots and oyster sauce.

Serves 4

500g (1 lb) rump steak cut into thin strips
4-6 small Chinese mushrooms
vegetable oil for deep frying
1 teaspoon grated fresh ginger
1 large spring onion, chopped
125g (4oz) mangetout
1 small carrot, thinly sliced
½ teaspoon soft brown sugar
¼ teaspoon salt
60 ml (2 fl oz) oyster sauce

Marinade
½ teaspoon soft brown sugar
1 tablespoon dark soy sauce
1 tablespoon Chinese rice wine
1 teaspoon cornflour
1 tablespoon vegetable oil

1 Mix all ingredients for the marinade together in a bowl. Add the beef and mix well to combine. Cover and leave in a cool place overnight.

2 Put mushrooms in a bowl. Cover with boiling water and leave for 20 minutes or until tender. Drain, remove stalks if necessary and dice mushrooms.

3 Heat about 2.5 cm (1 inch) oil in a wok or saucepan. Drain the beef and cook quickly in the hot oil for about 1 minute, stirring to separate the pieces. When colour of beef changes, remove and drain.

4 Pour off excess oil from the wok, leaving 2 tablespoons in the pan. Quickly stir-fry the mushrooms, ginger, spring onions, mangetout and carrot for 2-3 minutes. Add the sugar and salt and cook for a minute. Add the beef and oyster sauce and stir-fry for a minute or until heated through.

BEEF IN OYSTER SAUCE

CHINESE ROAST BEEF

EASY!

**Beef fillet marinated and then roasted and served
thinly sliced with chilli and plum sauces.**

Serves 6
1.5 kg (3 lb) beef fillet

Ginger Marinade
2 tablespoons soy sauce
2 tablespoons dry sherry
4 cloves garlic, finely chopped
1 teaspoon grated fresh ginger
2 teaspoons brown sugar

Dipping Sauce
3 tablespoons chilli sauce
3 tablespoons plum sauce

1 Tie beef to form an even shape and place in a shallow glass or ceramic dish.

2 To make marinade, place soy sauce, sherry, garlic, ginger and sugar in a small bowl and whisk to combine. Pour marinade over meat and turn to coat. Cover and set aside to marinate at room temperature for 3 hours or in the refrigerator overnight.

3 Preheat oven to 230C, 450F, Gas 8. If marinated overnight, bring beef to room temperature, drain, reserve marinade and place beef in a baking dish. Brush beef with marinade and bake in the preheated oven for 20 minutes, basting with additional marinade after 10 minutes. Remove beef from oven, cover and set aside to stand for 10 minutes.

4 To serve, slice beef and accompany with chilli and plum sauces for dipping.

BEEF WITH SPINACH

REALLY EASY!

A quick stir-fry of beef, spinach, cashew nuts and a satay and sherry sauce.

Serves 4
2 tablespoons peanut (groundnut) oil
500g (1 lb) lean rump steak, cut into strips
500g (1 lb) spinach, leaves removed and shredded
2 teaspoons grated fresh ginger
2 cloves garlic, crushed
3 teaspoons cornflour
250 ml (8 fl oz) water
2 tablespoons satay sauce
2 tablespoons dry sherry
1 tablespoon soy sauce
60g (2 oz) roasted cashew nuts

1 Heat oil in a wok or frying pan, add steak and stir-fry for 3-4 minutes or until browned. Remove meat from pan and drain on absorbent kitchen paper.

2 Add spinach, ginger and garlic to pan and stir-fry for 2-3 minutes or until spinach starts to wilt. Combine cornflour, water, satay sauce, sherry and soy sauce, stir into spinach mixture and cook for 2-3 minutes or until mixture boils and thickens.

3 Return meat to pan, add cashew nuts and cook for 2-3 minutes or until heated through.

CHINESE ROAST BEEF • BEEF WITH SPINACH

RED PEPPERED BEEF

REALLY EASY!

**Thin strips of beef speedily cooked with red
peppers, chilli, onion and garlic.**

Serves 4

500g (1 lb) lean rump steak, cut into thin strips
2 teaspoons cornflour
4 tablespoons soy sauce
3 tablespoons vegetable oil
2 red peppers, cut into thin strips
1 small fresh red chilli, finely chopped
3 spring onions, cut into 5 cm (2 inch) lengths
1 clove garlic, crushed
2 teaspoons grated fresh ginger
1 teaspoon sugar
2 tablespoons dry sherry

1 Place meat in a bowl, sprinkle with cornflour and
2 tablespoons soy sauce, toss to combine and set aside to
stand for 5 minutes.

2 Heat 1 tablespoon oil in a wok or frying pan, add red
peppers, chilli, spring onions, garlic and ginger and
stir-fry for 2-3 minutes. Remove vegetable mixture from
pan and set aside.

3 Heat remaining oil in pan, add meat and stir-fry for
2-3 minutes or until browned. Combine remaining soy
sauce, sugar and sherry. Return vegetable mixture to pan,
pour in soy sauce mixture and cook, stirring, for 1 minute
longer or until heated through.

SIMMERED BEEF

EASY!

A whole piece of topside gently braised in a stock flavoured with ginger, soy sauce, sherry and five spice powder.

Serves 6
1.5 kg (3 lb) piece topside
2 tablespoons peanut (groundnut) oil
1 clove garlic, crushed
2 teaspoons finely chopped fresh ginger
125 ml (4 fl oz) soy sauce
90 ml (3 fl oz) dry sherry
500 ml (16 fl oz) water
1 teaspoon five spice powder

1 Tie meat to form a neat shape that will hold during cooking.

2 Heat oil in a wok or large saucepan, add meat and brown on all sides. Add garlic, ginger, soy sauce, sherry, water and five spice powder to pan and bring to the boil. Cover, reduce heat and simmer, turning meat every 30 minutes for 1½ hours or until meat is tender.

3 To serve, remove string, slice meat and spoon over sauce.

BEEF AND NOODLES

REALLY EASY!

A filling dish of stir-fried beef, green pepper, sesame seeds and bean sprouts served on egg noodles.

Serves 4

250g (8 oz) egg noodles
1 tablespoon vegetable oil
500g (1 lb) lean rump steak, cut into strips
1 onion, sliced
1 clove garlic, crushed
½ green pepper, cut into strips
2 teaspoons oyster sauce
2 tablespoons sesame seeds, toasted
60g (2 oz) bean sprouts

1 Cook noodles in boiling water in a large saucepan following packet directions. Drain, set aside and keep warm.

2 Heat oil in a wok or frying pan, add beef and stir-fry for 3-4 minutes or until beef changes colour. Remove beef from pan and set aside.

3 Add onion, garlic and green pepper to pan and stir-fry for 5 minutes or until onion is soft. Return beef to pan, add oyster sauce, sesame seeds and bean sprouts and stir-fry for 2-3 minutes or until heated through. To serve, spoon beef mixture over noodles.

BEEF WITH BROCCOLI

EASY!

Thinly sliced rump steak stir-fried and served in a ring of tender broccoli florets.

Serves 6

500g (1 lb) lean rump steak, cut into paper thin slices
1 tablespoon soy sauce
1 tablespoon dry sherry
2 teaspoons grated fresh ginger
1 tablespoon vegetable oil
250 ml (8 fl oz) chicken stock
500g (1 lb) broccoli, broken into florets
2 teaspoons cornflour
2 teaspoons oyster sauce
2 teaspoons chilli sauce

1 Place meat, soy sauce, sherry and ginger in a bowl and mix to combine. Cover and set aside for 30 minutes.

2 Heat oil in a wok or large frying pan, add meat mixture and stir-fry for 4-5 minutes or until browned. Remove meat mixture from pan and set aside.

3 Add 125 ml (4 fl oz) stock to pan and bring to the boil. Add broccoli to stock, cover and cook for 5 minutes or until broccoli is tender. Drain and reserve stock. Place broccoli around edge of a serving platter, set aside and keep warm.

4 Combine cornflour, oyster sauce, chilli sauce and remaining stock, add to pan and bring to the boil. Return meat mixture to pan and cook, stirring, for 3-4 minutes or until heated through. Spoon meat mixture onto serving dish and serve at once.

SESAME BEEF WITH MANGETOUT

REALLY EASY!

A stir-fry of rump steak with mangetout and a light spicy sauce.

Serves 6-8

1kg (2 lb) rump steak, trimmed of all visible fat and cut into wide strips
30g (1 oz) cornflour
2 teaspoons vegetable oil
1 teaspoon sesame oil
2 tablespoons soy sauce
2 tablespoons oyster sauce
2 tablespoons hoisin sauce
300g (10 oz) mangetout
3 tablespoons toasted sesame seeds

1 Toss steak in cornflour to coat, shake off excess and set aside.

2 Heat a wok or large frying pan over a high heat. Add vegetable and sesame oils and steak and stir-fry for 2 minutes. Stir in soy sauce, oyster sauce and hoisin sauce and stir-fry for 1 minute longer.

3 Add mangetout and sesame seeds and stir-fry for 1 minute or until mangetout are just cooked. Serve immediately.

BEEF IN BEAN SAUCE

REALLY EASY!

Beef stir-fried with red pepper, bean sprouts and mangetout, and moistened with a black bean sauce.

Serves 4

1 tablespoon vegetable oil
1 clove garlic, crushed
1 tablespoon grated fresh ginger
1 onion, finely sliced
350g (12 oz) lean rump steak, cut into strips
2 teaspoons sesame oil
½ red pepper, sliced
90g (3 oz) bean sprouts
60g (2 oz) mangetout
2 tablespoons black bean sauce
1 tablespoon soy sauce
60 ml (2 fl oz) beef stock
1 teaspoon sugar
1 teaspoon cornflour blended with 1 tablespoon water

1 Heat vegetable oil in a wok or frying pan, add garlic and ginger and stir-fry for 1 minute. Add onion and beef and stir-fry for 3 minutes or until beef is browned. Remove meat mixture from pan and set aside.

2 Heat sesame oil in pan, add red pepper, bean sprouts and mangetout and stir-fry for 1 minute. Add black bean sauce, soy sauce, stock, sugar and cornflour mixture and cook, stirring, until mixture thickens slightly. Return meat mixture to pan and cook for 2-3 minutes longer or until heated through.

VEGETABLES AND VEGETARIAN DISHES

The most delicious Western vegetarian cooking owes much to Chinese cooks who have been practising the art for thousands of years. The Chinese style of cooking vegetables is quite unique, they are tossed in hot oil over a very high heat for a minimum of time. The vegetables are colourful, crunchy and keep most of their vitamins and so are very nutritious. Always buy fresh crisp produce and only wash and cut them just before cooking to retain as much goodness as possible. Tasty, colourful and nutritious, these recipes are sure to become popular favourites at your table.

SAUTÉED CHINESE GREENS

REALLY EASY!

A mixture of Chinese greens chopped and quickly stir-fried with black bean paste, garlic and oyster sauce.

Serves 6-8

300g (10 oz) pak choi (Chinese cabbage)
300g (10 oz) Chinese broccoli
300g (10 oz) Chinese leaves
1 tablespoon vegetable oil
2 teaspoons black bean paste
2 cloves garlic, crushed
3 tablespoons oyster sauce
2 tablespoons water

1 Trim thick stalks from pak choi, broccoli and cabbage. Discard stalks and chop leaves into large pieces.

2 Heat wok or large frying pan over a medium heat. Add oil, black bean paste, garlic, oyster sauce and water and stir-fry for 2 minutes.

3 Add vegetables and stir-fry for 2 minutes or until leaves are just wilted.

BRAISED BAMBOO SHOOTS

REALLY EASY!

Bamboo shoots stir-fried with onions, red pepper, sherry, soy sauce and sesame seeds.

Serves 4
1 tablespoon vegetable oil
1 onion, sliced
1 red pepper, diced
400g (14 oz) canned bamboo shoots, drained and thinly sliced
1 tablespoon sesame seeds, toasted
1 tablespoon dry sherry
2 teaspoons soy sauce

1 Heat oil in a wok or frying pan, add onion and red pepper and stir-fry for 4-5 minutes or until onion is soft.

2 Add bamboo shoots, sesame seeds, sherry and soy sauce and stir-fry for 3-4 minutes longer or until heated through. Serve immediately.

SESAME CABBAGE

R E A L L Y   E A S Y !

**Chinese cabbage, bean sprouts and
chillies, stir-fried in sesame oil.**

Serves 4
1 tablespoon sesame oil
1 onion, chopped
60g (2 oz) bean sprouts
½ pak choi (Chinese cabbage), chopped
2 fresh red chillies, chopped
60 ml (2 fl oz) water
freshly ground black pepper

1 Heat oil in a wok or frying pan, add onion and stir-fry
for 4-5 minutes or until soft.

2 Add bean sprouts, cabbage, chillies and water and
stir-fry for 4-5 minutes longer or until cabbage is tender.
Season to taste with black pepper and serve immediately.

BRAISED BAMBOO SHOOTS • SESAME CABBAGE

BRAISED GREEN VEGETABLES

REALLY EASY!

**Broccoli, celery, spinach and mangetout
stir-fried and then cooked with a little chicken
stock until tender.**

Serves 6
2 tablespoons vegetable oil
1 tablespoon grated fresh ginger
2 onions, cut into wedges and separated
500g (1 lb) broccoli, broken into florets
4 stalks celery, diagonally sliced
6 large spinach leaves, chopped
250g (8 oz) mangetout
150 ml (5 fl oz) chicken stock
freshly ground black pepper
8 spring onions, diagonally sliced

1 Heat oil in a wok or frying pan, add ginger and onions and stir-fry for 2-3 minutes. Add broccoli and celery and stir-fry for 2-3 minutes longer.

2 Add spinach and mangetout and stir-fry for 2-3 minutes. Stir in chicken stock and bring to the boil. Reduce heat, cover pan and simmer 4-5 minutes or until vegetables are just tender. Add spring onions and serve immediately.

GARLIC BEANS

REALLY EASY!

Green beans boiled until tender then drained and quickly stir-fried with garlic and spring onions.

Serves 4
250 ml (8 fl oz) chicken stock
250g (8 oz) green beans
1 tablespoon vegetable oil
2 cloves garlic, crushed
4 spring onions, diagonally sliced
2 teaspoons soy sauce
1 teaspoon sesame oil

1 Place stock in a saucepan and bring to the boil. Add beans and cook for 10 minutes or until tender. Drain and refresh under cold running water.

2 Heat vegetable oil in a wok or frying pan, add garlic and spring onions and stir-fry for 1 minute. Add beans, soy sauce and sesame oil and stir-fry for 2-3 minutes or until heated through. Serve immediately.

BRAISED GREEN VEGETABLES • GARLIC BEANS

135

STEAMED VEGETARIAN BUNS

**A light bun dough filled with a mixture
of tofu, mushrooms, carrot and peas
and then steamed.**

Makes 12
4 dried Chinese mushrooms
1 tablespoon vegetable oil
2 cloves garlic, crushed
30g (1 oz) button mushrooms, diced
1 small carrot, diced
60g (2 oz) firm tofu, diced
30g (1 oz) fresh or frozen peas
1 tablespoon oyster sauce
½ teaspoon sugar
½ teaspoon freshly ground black pepper
¼ teaspoon salt
12 x 5 cm (2 inches) square pieces non-stick baking paper

Bun Dough
180g (6 oz) self-raising flour
½ teaspoon baking powder
60g (2 oz) sugar
pinch salt
125 ml (4 fl oz) water
1 tablespoon vegetable oil
1 teaspoon vinegar

1 Place Chinese mushrooms in a bowl, cover with boiling water and set aside to soak for 20 minutes or until mushrooms are tender. Drain, remove stalks if necessary and chop mushrooms.

2 Heat oil in a wok or frying pan over a medium heat, add Chinese mushrooms, garlic, button mushrooms, carrot and tofu and stir-fry for 4-5 minutes or until vegetables are almost cooked. Add peas, oyster sauce, sugar, black pepper and salt and stir-fry for 2-3 minutes longer or until heated through. Remove pan from heat and set aside to cool completely.

3 To make dough, sift flour and baking powder together into a large bowl, add sugar and salt and mix to combine. Add water, oil and vinegar and mix to form a soft dough. Turn dough onto a lightly-floured surface and knead for 5-10 minutes or until dough is smooth. Cover and set aside to rest for 15 minutes.

4 Divide dough into 12 portions and working on a lightly-floured surface, roll each portion into a ball. Lightly flatten each ball of dough to make a 10 cm (4 inch) round. Place a spoonful of filling in the centre of each dough round and brush the edges with water. Draw pastry around mixture and pinch together to form a bun.

5 Place bun, join side down, on a piece of the baking paper and place in a bamboo steamer. Repeat with remaining dough rounds and filling to use all ingredients.

6 Cover steamer with lid, place over a saucepan of simmering water and steam for 15-20 minutes or until buns are cooked through.

STEAMED VEGETARIAN BUNS

CHILLI VEGETABLES

REALLY EASY!

Aubergines, mushrooms and peas, cooked with chillies, garlic and yellow bean paste sauce.

Serves 4

¼ teaspoon sugar
½ teaspoon salt
½ teaspoon sesame oil
1 tablespoon yellow bean paste
125 ml (4 fl oz) water
60 ml (2 fl oz) vegetable oil
2 aubergines, cut into chunks
2 large mushrooms, quartered
2 large oyster mushrooms, sliced
2 cm (¾ inch) piece peeled fresh ginger, grated
2 cloves garlic, crushed
2 fresh red chillies, finely chopped
30g (1 oz) fresh or frozen peas

1 Place sugar, salt, sesame oil, bean paste and water in a small bowl, mix to combine and set aside.

2 Heat 2 tablespoons vegetable oil in a wok or frying pan over a medium heat, add aubergines and cook, turning frequently, until they begin to soften. Add more oil if needed. Remove aubergines from pan and set aside.

3 Heat remaining vegetable oil in pan, add mushrooms, oyster mushrooms, ginger, garlic and chillies and stir-fry for 2-3 minutes.

4 Add bean paste mixture to pan and toss to coat all ingredients. Add aubergines and peas to pan and stir-fry for 2-3 minutes or until heated through.

SWEET AND SOUR TOFU

REALLY EASY!

Tofu or bean curd has been an important ingredient in Chinese and Japanese cuisines for over 1000 years.

Serves 4
1 tablespoon peanut (groundnut) oil
250g (8 oz) firm tofu, cut into 2.5 cm (1 inch) cubes
1 red pepper, cut into thin strips
2 carrots, cut into thin strips
150g (5 oz) mangetout
2 teaspoons grated fresh ginger
1 clove garlic, crushed
300g (10 oz) canned pineapple pieces, drained and juice reserved
90 ml (3 fl oz) water
1 tablespoon cornflour
1 tablespoon vinegar

1 Heat oil in a wok or frying pan, add tofu and stir-fry for 4-5 minutes or until golden. Remove tofu from pan and set aside.

2 Add red pepper, carrots, mangetout, ginger and garlic to pan and stir-fry for 3 minutes.

3 Measure reserved pineapple juice to make up 250 ml (8 fl oz) – if there is insufficient juice, make up quantity with water. Combine pineapple juice, water, cornflour and vinegar, add to vegetable mixture and cook, stirring constantly, for 3-4 minutes or until sauce thickens and boils.

4 Add tofu and pineapple pieces to pan and cook for 2-3 minutes longer or until heated through.

TOMATO AND CHILLI OMELETTE

REALLY EASY!

An omelette with added tomato, onion and chillies.

Serves 1
2 eggs
¼ teaspoon salt
½ tomato, finely chopped
½ onion, finely chopped
½ fresh red chilli, seeded and finely chopped
½ fresh green chilli, seeded and finely chopped
1 tablespoon vegetable oil

1 Place eggs and salt in a bowl and whisk to combine. Add tomato, onion and chillies and mix to combine. Heat oil in a small non-stick frying pan over a medium heat, add egg mixture and swirl to coat pan. Cook until omelette just begins to set. Fold omelette in half, then in half again. Slide onto serving plate and serve immediately.

EGG AND TOFU FRIED RICE

REALLY EASY!

Rice for fried rice should be completely cold before using – it is best to cook the rice the day before, then to chill it overnight.

Serves 2
2½ tablespoons vegetable oil
125g (4 oz) firm tofu, diced
3 eggs, lightly beaten
300g (10 oz) long grain rice, cooked and cooled
60g (2 oz)green beans, chopped
¼ teaspoon salt
¼ teaspoon freshly ground black pepper
2 teaspoons light soy sauce

1 Heat 1 tablespoon oil in a wok or frying pan over a medium heat, add tofu and stir-fry for 2-3 minutes or until golden. Remove tofu from pan. Set aside.

2 Heat ½ tablespoon oil in pan. Pour eggs into pan, swirl to coat pan evenly and cook over a low heat until omelette is just set. Chop and set aside.

3 Add remaining oil and rice to pan and stir-fry for 3-4 minutes to separate grains. Add beans, salt, black pepper and soy sauce to pan and stir-fry for 3-4 minutes until beans are just cooked. Return tofu and omelette strips to pan and toss to combine.

RICE AND NOODLES

Whether fried or steamed, noodles
and rice are an essential addition to a Chinese
meal. Rice cooked to accompany a Chinese meal
can be fluffy or slightly sticky and glutinous,
either is perfectly acceptable. It is best to use a
long grain rice such as Basmati, if you want fluffy
rice. For a stickier rice that is easy to pick up
with chopsticks, use Patna or short grain rice,
and for very sticky rice use Thai or Japanese
rice. Noodles can be bought fresh or dried and
are very quick to cook. You can choose from Egg
Noodles – made from wheatflour and eggs, Wheat
Noodles – made from wheat flour and water,
Cellophane Noodles – made from the paste of the
green soya bean, or Rice Noodles – made from
rice flour dough.

CHINESE FRIED RICE

REALLY EASY!

Cooked rice stir-fried with spring onions, mushrooms, red and green pepper, prawns and ham.

Serves 4

2 tablespoons vegetable oil
6 spring onions, chopped
125g (4 oz) mushrooms, chopped
½ red pepper, chopped
½ green pepper, chopped
200g (7 oz) long grain rice, cooked and cooled
250g (8 oz) cooked prawns, peeled and deveined
125g (4 oz) ham, diced
½ teaspoon ground ginger
¼ teaspoon Cayenne pepper

1 Heat oil in a wok or frying pan, add spring onions, mushrooms and red and green pepper and stir-fry for 2-3 minutes.

2 Add rice and stir-fry for 3 minutes longer.

3 Add prawns, ham, ginger and cayenne pepper and stir-fry for 3-4 minutes longer or until heated through.

FRAGRANT STEAMED RICE

EASY!

**Long grain rice cooked with minced
pork, mushrooms, shrimps and
Chinese cabbage.**

Serves 4-6

½ teaspoon sugar
1 teaspoon salt
½ teaspoon freshly ground black pepper
½ teaspoon sesame oil
1½ tablespoons light soy sauce
2 tablespoons vegetable oil
200g (7 oz) lean pork mince
5 dried Chinese mushrooms
45g (1½ oz) dried shrimps
1 clove garlic, crushed
6 stalks pak choi, (Chinese cabbage) chopped
300g (10 oz) long grain rice, washed and drained
500 ml (16 fl oz) water

1 Place sugar, ½ teaspoon salt, black pepper, sesame oil, soy sauce and 1 tablespoon vegetable oil in a bowl and mix to combine. Add pork, mix to combine and set aside to marinate for 10-15 minutes.

2 Place mushrooms in a bowl, cover with boiling water and set aside to soak for 20 minutes or until mushrooms are tender. Drain, remove stalks if necessary and chop.

3 Remove any pieces of shell from shrimps. Place shrimps in a bowl, cover with hot water and set aside to soak for 10-15 minutes or until shrimps are tender. Drain and reserve soaking water.

4 Heat remaining vegetable oil in a wok or frying pan over a medium heat, add shrimps and stir-fry for 1-2 minutes. Add pork mixture, garlic, mushrooms, pak choi, reserved shrimp soaking water, rice and remaining salt and stir-fry for 3-4 minutes.

5 Transfer mixture to a large saucepan, stir in water and bring to the boil. Reduce heat to low, cover and cook for 15-20 minutes or until liquid is absorbed and rice is tender.

SPECIAL FRIED RICE

EASY!

**Cooked rice with Chinese Sausage,
barbecued pork, prawns and shredded omelette.**

Serves 4
4 tablespoons vegetable oil
2 eggs, lightly beaten with ¼ teaspoon salt
*45g (1½ oz) Chinese sausage (Lap Cheong), cut into
1 cm (½ inch) pieces*
125g (4 oz) small uncooked prawns, peeled and deveined
300g (10 oz) long grain rice, cooked and cooled
1½ tablespoons light soy sauce
½ teaspoon salt
*125g (4 oz) Chinese barbecued pork or Chinese roast
pork, thinly sliced*
2 spring onions, chopped

1 Heat 1 tablespoon oil in wok or frying pan over a low heat, pour egg mixture into pan, swirl to coat pan evenly and cook for 2-3 minutes or until omelette is set. As omelette cooks cut it into pieces using a spatula. Remove from pan and set aside.

2 Heat pan over a low heat, add sausage and stir-fry for 4-5 minutes or until crisp. Remove sausage from pan and set aside. Add 1 tablespoon oil and prawns to pan and stir-fry for 2 minutes or until they just change colour. Remove prawns from pan and set aside.

3 Heat remaining oil in pan, add rice and stir-fry for 3-4 minutes to separate grains. Add soy sauce and salt and stir-fry for 1-2 minutes. Add pork and return omelette, sausage and prawns to pan and stir-fry for 3-4 minutes or until heated through. Remove pan from heat, add spring onions and toss to combine.

FRIED BROWN RICE

REALLY EASY!

V

**While not traditional - the Chinese do not use
brown rice - this version of fried rice is delicious.
You can, of course, use white rice if you prefer.**

Serves 4
300g (10 oz) brown rice
2 tablespoons peanut (groundnut) oil
2 stalks celery, chopped
1 red pepper, chopped
2 cloves garlic, crushed
2 eggs, lightly beaten
60g (2 oz) peas, cooked
4 spring onions, chopped
1 tablespoon soy sauce

1 Cook rice in boiling water until tender. Drain, spread out on a tray and refrigerate until cold.

2 Heat oil in a wok or frying pan, add celery, red pepper and garlic and stir-fry for 4-5 minutes or until vegetables are just tender. Remove vegetables from pan and set aside.

3 Pour eggs into pan and cook over a low heat, stirring, until eggs are set. Chop roughly and set aside.

4 Add rice to pan and stir-fry to separate grains. Return vegetable mixture and eggs to pan, add peas, spring onions and soy sauce and stir-fry for 3-4 minutes or until heated through.

SPECIAL FRIED RICE • FRIED BROWN RICE

147

GARLIC NOODLES WITH SEAFOOD

E A S Y !

This dish is delicious accompanied by sliced red chillies or pickled green chillies.

Serves 4

125g (4 oz) medium uncooked prawns, peeled and deveined
1¼ teaspoons sugar
salt
freshly ground black pepper
500g (1 lb)fresh round egg noodles
90 ml (3 fl oz) vegetable oil
2 tablespoons oyster sauce
4 cloves garlic, finely chopped
125g (4 oz) prepared scallops
60g (2 oz) squid rings
5 stalks pak choi (chinese cabbage)
½ teaspoon sesame oil
½ teaspoon light soy sauce
125 ml (4 fl oz) water blended with 1 teaspoon cornflour and 1 teaspoon chicken stock powder
2 tablespoons chopped fresh coriander

1 Combine prawns, ¼ teaspoon sugar and salt and black pepper to taste in a bowl and marinate for 10-15 minutes.

2 Cook noodles in boiling water in a large saucepan, following packet directions. Drain well and rinse under cold running water. Turn noodles onto absorbent kitchen paper and pat dry.

3 Heat 2 tablespoons vegetable oil in a wok or frying pan over a medium heat, add noodles, oyster sauce, half the garlic and ½ teaspoon sugar and stir-fry for 3-4 minutes or until garlic is golden. Remove from pan, set aside and keep warm.

4 Heat remaining vegetable oil in pan, add prawns, scallops, squid, pak choi and remaining garlic and stir-fry for 5 minutes or until seafood is almost cooked. Stir in remaining sugar, sesame oil, soy sauce, ¼ teaspoon salt, ¼ teaspoon black pepper and cornflour mixture and bring to the boil. To serve, place noodles on a serving platter, top with seafood mixture and sprinkle with coriander.

GARLIC NOODLES WITH SEAFOOD

FRIED NOODLES WITH PORK

EASY!

Rice noodles with strips of belly pork, prawns and shredded omelette.

Serves 4

250g (8 oz) rice noodles (vermicelli)
light soy sauce
1 teaspoon salt
½ teaspoon sugar
1 teaspoon sesame oil
¼ teaspoon freshly ground black pepper
¼ teaspoon cornflour
125g (4 oz) pork belly, cut into 3 cm (1¼ inch) strips
vegetable oil
2 eggs, lightly beaten
2 teaspoons oyster sauce
60g (2 oz) small uncooked prawns, peeled and deveined
½ carrot, cut into 3 cm (1¼ inch) strips
8 fresh chives, cut into 2.5 cm (1 inch) pieces
1 clove garlic, crushed

1 Cook noodles in boiling water in a large saucepan following packet directions. Drain and set aside.

2 Place 1 teaspoon soy sauce, ¼ teaspoon salt, sugar, ½ teaspoon sesame oil, black pepper and cornflour in a bowl and mix to combine. Add pork, toss to combine and set aside to marinate for 10-15 minutes.

3 Heat 1 tablespoon vegetable oil in wok or frying pan over a medium heat, pour eggs into pan, swirl to coat pan evenly and cook for 2-3 minutes or until omelette is set and golden on the base. Turn omelette onto a board, roll up, cut into strips and set aside.

4 Place 1 tablespoon soy sauce, remaining sesame oil,

remaining salt and oyster sauce in a small bowl and mix to combine. Set aside.

5 Heat 1 tablespoon vegetable oil in pan over a medium heat, add pork and stir-fry for 4-5 minutes or until pork changes colour. Remove pork from pan and set aside.

6 Heat 1 tablespoon vegetable oil in pan over a medium heat, add prawns and stir-fry for 2 minutes or until prawns just change colour. Remove prawns from pan and set aside.

7 Heat 1 tablespoon vegetable oil in pan, add noodles, carrot, chives and garlic to pan and stir-fry for 2-3 minutes. Add oyster sauce mixture, omelette, pork and prawns to pan and stir-fry for 2-3 minutes or until heated through.

FRIED NOODLES WITH PORK

CHILLI SOY NOODLES

EASY!

To make ginger oil, put 1 litre (1¾ pints) vegetable oil and 1 cm (½ inch) piece of peeled fresh ginger in a saucepan. Bring just to a simmer over a medium heat. Remove, cool and then strain and store in a bottle until required.

Serves 2

2½ tablespoons ginger oil
1½ tablespoons oyster sauce
1 tablespoon chilli sauce
1 teaspoon light soy sauce
¼ teaspoon sesame oil
3 x 75g (2½ oz) cakes instant noodles

1 Place ginger oil, oyster sauce, chilli sauce, soy sauce and sesame oil in a bowl and mix to combine. Set aside.

2 Prepare noodles following packet directions. Drain well. Add sauce to noodles and toss to combine. Serve immediately.

DESSERTS

It is not the custom in China to serve puddings or sweet dishes with every-day meals and so there is only a limited range of Chinese desserts. You can always end the meal with a fruit salad served in a melon shell or fresh or canned lychees or even ice cream. However, you may wish to conclude your Chinese meal and impress guests and family with one of these special desserts. These recipes, including Pandan Chiffon Cake and Fruit Salad with Almond Jelly, taste every bit as good as they sound.

CUSTARD TARTS

EASY!

Shortcrust pastry tarts with a creamy custard filling.

Makes 24 tarts
350g (12 oz) prepared shortcrust pastry
125g (4 oz) sugar
180 ml (6 fl oz) water
3 eggs, lightly beaten
90 ml (3 fl oz) milk

1 Roll out pastry to 3 mm (⅛ inch) thick and, using an 8 cm (3¼ inch) cutter, cut out 24 circles. Press pastry circles into lightly greased shallow patty tins (tartlet tins).

2 Place sugar and water in a saucepan and cook over a medium heat without boiling, stirring constantly until sugar is dissolved. Remove pan from heat and set aside to cool. Preheat oven to 200C, 400F, Gas 6.

3 Add eggs and milk to sugar syrup and mix to combine. Pour egg mixture into pastry cases and bake in the preheated oven for 10 minutes, then reduce oven temperature to 180C, 350F, Gas 4 and cook for 10 minutes longer or until custard is set.

SESAME TOFFEE APPLES

While this dish takes a little time to prepare and cook, it is well worth the effort. Other fruits, such as bananas and oranges, are also delicious cooked in this way.

Serves 6
6 apples, cored, peeled and quartered
30g (1 oz) flour
1 tablespoon cornflour
2 egg whites
vegetable oil for deep-frying

Sesame Toffee
250g (8 oz) sugar
90 ml (3 fl oz) water
1 tablespoon sesame seeds

1 Dust apples with a little of the flour. Place remaining flour and cornflour in a bowl, stir in egg whites and mix to make a smooth batter.

2 Heat oil in a deep saucepan until a cube of bread, when dropped in, browns in 50 seconds. Dip apple pieces in batter and cook a few at a time in oil until golden. Drain on absorbent kitchen paper.

3 To make toffee, place sugar and water in a saucepan and cook over a medium heat, stirring constantly, without boiling, until sugar is dissolved. Bring sugar syrup to the boil, without stirring, and cook until syrup turns a light golden colour. Remove pan from heat and stir in sesame seeds.

4 Dip apple pieces into hot syrup then drop into a bowl of iced water to set the toffee. Remove and serve warm.

STEAMED BANANA CAKE

EASY!

**Green mung pea flour, often labelled as
tepung juan kwe, is available from Oriental
food stores. If it is unavailable, arrowroot is a
suitable substitute, however the flavour
will be a little different.**

Makes 30
2 ripe bananas
60g (2 oz) green mung pea flour or arrowroot
125g (4 oz) sugar
pinch salt
560 ml (18 fl oz) coconut milk
180 ml (6 fl oz) water
red food colouring

1 Place bananas with skins on in steamer, set over a saucepan of simmering water and steam for 5-8 minutes or until bananas are soft. Remove from steamer and set aside to cool. Peel bananas, dice and set aside.

2 Place flour or arrowroot, sugar and salt in a bowl and mix to combine. Combine coconut milk and water and slowly stir into flour. Strain mixture into a saucepan and cook, stirring constantly, over a medium heat for 8-10 minutes or until mixture boils and thickens.

3 Remove pan from heat and pour half the mixture into a 15 x 23 cm (6 x 9 inch) glass or ceramic dish rinsed in cold water. Top with bananas. Colour remaining coconut milk mixture with food colouring. Spoon over bananas, set aside to cool and set. To serve, cut into diamond shapes.

FRUIT SALAD WITH ALMOND JELLY

EASY!

Agar agar is an extract of seaweed and is used by vegetarians instead of gelatine.

Serves 10-12
2½ teaspoons agar agar powder
60g (2 oz) caster sugar
500 ml (16 fl oz) water
½ teaspoon almond essence
75 ml (2½ fl oz) evaporated milk
400g (14 oz) canned fruit salad
400g (14 oz) canned lychees

1 Place agar agar powder, sugar and a little water in a bowl and mix to dissolve agar agar. Place remaining water in a saucepan and bring to the boil over a medium heat. Lower heat, stir in agar agar mixture and cook, stirring constantly, for 5 minutes.

2 Remove pan from heat, stir in almond essence and evaporated milk and mix well to combine. Pour mixture into a shallow 20 cm (8 inch) square cake tin and refrigerate until set. To serve, place fruit salad and lychees with juice in a large bowl. Cut jelly into bite-sized wedges or cubes and add to fruit mixture. Chill until ready to serve.

STEAMED BANANA CAKE • FRUIT SALAD WITH ALMOND JELLY

PANDAN CHIFFON CAKE

EASY!

Serves 8

180g (6 oz) plain flour
3 teaspoons baking powder
8 eggs, separated
½ teaspoon cream of tartar
280g (9 oz) caster sugar
125 ml (4 fl oz) vegetable oil
180 ml (6 fl oz) coconut milk
1 teaspoon pandan essence

1 Sift together flour and baking powder three times and set aside.

2 Place egg whites and cream of tartar in a bowl, beat until stiff peaks form. Set aside.

3 Preheat oven to 180C, 350F, Gas 4. Place egg yolks and sugar in a bowl and beat until light and fluffy. Stir in oil, coconut milk and pandan essence. Fold in flour mixture and mix well to combine. Using a metal spoon, fold egg white mixture into egg yolk mixture in batches.

4 Spoon batter into an ungreased 23 cm (9 inch) ring tin and bake in the preheated oven for 45 minutes. Stand cake in tin for 5 minutes before turning onto a wire rack to cool.

INDEX